THE MORMON TABERNACLE ORGAN

ORGAN

AN AMERICAN CLASSIC

THE MORMON TABERNACLE ORGAN

AN AMERICAN CLASSIC

BY
BARBARA
OWEN

THE AMERICAN CLASSIC
ORGAN SYMPOSIUM

TEMPLE SQUARE

SALT LAKE CITY, UTAH

ISBN 1-55517-054-4
Library of Congress Catalog Card No. 90-81240

The American Classic Organ Symposium
expresses its deep gratitude to The James LeVoy Sorenson Foundation
for the generous grant that
enabled this definitive treatise on the
Tabernacle organ to
be published.

Printed by Paragon Press, Salt Lake City, Utah   Bound by Hiller Industries, Salt Lake City, Utah

Contents

List of Illustrations

Unless listed below, black-and-white photographs are courtesy of the Historical Department or Visual Resources Library of The Church of Jesus Christ of Latter-day Saints. Color photographs are by Jed A. Clark, head of Photo Services of The Church of Jesus Christ of Latter-day Saints.

Page 4 courtesy of the Joseph J. Daynes family
Page 24 courtesy of the Leland Van Wagoner family
Page 36 courtesy of the *Deseret News*
Page 59 photo of Steuart Goodwin by Howard Woodall
Page 61 John Luke (LDS Photo Services)
Page 76 courtesy of the Board of Trustees of the Methuen Memorial Music Hall, Inc.
Page 110 Craig Dimond (LDS Photo Services)

Preface

In 1989 almost 4,500,000 people came to Temple Square in Salt Lake City, making it the fifth most-visited tourist attraction in the United States. For more than 120 years visitors from around the world have assembled here for worship and for music. Audiences of as many as 3,000 hear the daily organ recitals in the Tabernacle. And on summer Sundays, capacity audiences exceeding 5,000 often gather to hear the Tabernacle Choir in its weekly CBS broadcast of "Music and the Spoken Word." Additional millions of people see and hear this broadcast on television and radio.

Much has already been written about the Tabernacle and the Choir. But the story of the Tabernacle organ has not been fully told. How did this organ evolve from pioneer times to the present? What is it about this organ that has drawn international praise and acclaim? What kind of organ is needed to meet such diverse musical needs? As this volume examines these questions, it reflects, in microcosm, a cross-section of American organ history.

As we write this preface we are poignantly aware of the constant change the passage of time brings. We have just learned that at Brigham Young University, the Joseph Smith Building is slated for demolition. For nearly half a century this building has housed the Austin organ that formerly stood in the Salt Lake Tabernacle. Although the organ's pipes will be salvaged and carefully stored with the promise that appropriate ranks will be included in a future rebuilding of the organ, this honored link with our past will be silenced for some time. This unforeseen development at Brigham Young University makes us doubly aware of the need for this book. We are now especially grateful for Barbara Owen's careful research and documentation of the Austin organ.

The concern for ensuring constancy in a changing world applies especially to pipe organs. These instruments are often victims of changing musical tastes, the devastation of war and natural catastrophes, and the uncertain future of the buildings in which they are housed. Pipe organs potentially can function for hundreds of years but often meet their end while still in their youth.

Three criteria are especially important for pipe organ longevity. First, the instrument should be an outstanding representation of the style in which it is built. Second, the instrument should be housed in a building that complements the organ and is of corresponding significance. Third, the instrument and the building should both meet the basic needs of their users.

While the Tabernacle and its organ meet the first two criteria, some people may question whether it meets the third. However, the period of time from the installation of the Æolian-Skinner organ in 1948 until the renovation in 1984-88 represents the longest period thus far when no significant changes were made in the Tabernacle organ. Moreover, the renovation was of modest scope when compared to the changes that occurred in the Tabernacle organs before 1944. We are confident that the thoughtful reader will share our conviction that the present instrument fulfills admirably the varied musical tasks required of it.

More than a year has passed since the Tabernacle organ's renovation was completed, and our original enthusiasm for the success of the project remains undiminished. As we travel to other locations throughout the world, we inevitably compare this organ with other distinguished instruments. Always we return home with heightened gratitude for the beauty and utility of the Tabernacle organ. We are most blessed to serve in the special musical ministry at Temple Square with an organ that is truly "an American classic."

Robert Cundick

John Longhurst

Clay Christiansen

The Tabernacle

Temple Square

Salt Lake City, Utah

April 1990

Acknowledgments

Crucial to the completeness of any historical research project is the assistance of friends and colleagues. In this I have been extraordinarily fortunate, for the outcome of this study would have been much the poorer without the enthusiastic assistance of Jack Bethards, who initiated the idea, read the first draft, and contributed his detailed description of the Æolian-Skinner organ; the Tabernacle organists—Robert Cundick, John Longhurst, and Clay Christiansen— who took time from their busy schedules to make arrangements with the Church Archives, read the first draft, and contribute material; Robert Poll, Tabernacle organ technician, who researched and contributed technical material, provided an informative tour of the Tabernacle organ, and read the first draft; Warren Luch for the design, Jon Killpack for the typesetting, Andrew Olsen for the editing, and Jed Clark for the color photography. Thanks are also due to Parley L. Belnap and Douglas L. Bush of Brigham Young University for their insights and for arranging a survey of the Provo organ; to Ronald G. Watt and Pauline Koch Musig of the LDS Historical Department for finding important information on short notice, and to William C. Parsons of the Library of Congress and Stephen Pinel of the Organ Historical Society for the same; to Floyd T. Higgins and Eric Ezequelle of Austin Organs, Inc., for searching out and sending valuable information from the company files; to Allen Kinzey for copies of pertinent material from the Æolian-Skinner records; to Davis Bitton for reading the first draft; to Edgar V. Orth for sharing his research; and to Nelson Barden for clarifying some puzzling technical matters. I hope that all will see a little of their own contribution in this monograph.

Barbara Owen
Newburyport, Mass.
April 1990

JOSEPH RIDGES

Prologue

In the summer of 1847, after weeks of grueling travel with wagons and handcarts along the Platte River and across the Rocky Mountains, a band of Mormon pioneers under the leadership of Brigham Young reached the desolate Salt Lake Valley. There, at the foot of the snow-crowned mountains, they planted the settlement that was to become Salt Lake City.

Building shelters and sowing crops were the first order of business for these settlers. It is recorded that less than a month after they arrived they had organized a choir—the precursor of today's famed Mormon Tabernacle Choir. Within a few years, choirs and bands from other Mormon settlements were coming to Salt Lake City for musical competitions.[1] By 1852 the first Tabernacle, a barnlike structure with thick adobe walls and a pine-shingled roof, was completed. This building, now referred to as the Old Tabernacle, was used not only for services and lectures, but also for musical events, since music played an important part in the lives of these people. A decade later, the Deseret Musical Association was "organized for the purpose of diffusing throughout the territory a taste for the cultivation of music upon rational and scientific principles" and held its first concert in the Old Tabernacle.[2]

In the fall of 1851, half a world away from the embryonic settlement in frontier Utah, Joseph Ridges, an English house carpenter, and his family embarked on a sailing vessel bound for Australia. Gold had been discovered, and a carpenter could find plenty of work in the fast-growing town of Sydney if he did not find gold as well.

Joseph Harris Ridges's birthplace is variously cited as Eling, a small town west of Southampton,[3] or Ealing, a western suburb of London,[4] but the former is confirmed by the Family History Library of The Church of Jesus Christ of Latter-day Saints. According to an entry in the register of the Totton Independent Church of Eling, Hampshire, Ridges was born on April 25, 1827, the son of Edward and Rebecca Ridges.[5] His family must have moved to London when he was a child, however, for in an interview given late in his life, Ridges referred to London as the place where his lifelong interest in organs was kindled:

> Across the street where I lived when a boy near London was a pair of massive, tall iron fretwork gates. Beyond them was situated a large organ loft and factory. I can remember those youthful days in green England, and the delight with which I used to sometimes pass beyond those gates and revel in the mysteries of that organ factory and watch the men at their work, and study and think out the purposes and uses of the numerous things the mechanics were at work upon.[6]

The Ridges family may have lived in the St. Pancras District, near the heart of London, for it was in that district that the marriage of Joseph Ridges to Adelaide Whitely was recorded in 1850.[7] Through the middle of this district ran Euston Road, only a few blocks long (although part of a much longer thoroughfare), which was the location of several organ factories in this period, notably those of William Hill, Thomas Harrison, and Henry Willis. Hill's establishment would have been the largest of these during the years of Ridges's youth and may well have been the one that Ridges once explored with a "youthful chum," who seems to have been an organ builder's apprentice.

This interest in organs often prompted Ridges to walk many miles in the hope of being allowed to examine the interior of some interesting organ. Despite this interest, Ridges became a carpenter rather than an organ builder. Two years after his marriage, Ridges, by his own admission "suffering from a bad attack of gold fever," set out for Australia with his wife and infant son.

Among their companions for the five-month voyage were Luke and Christiana Syphus, who were Mormons. When the ship arrived at Australia, Ridges and Syphus trekked 400 miles into the bush in search of the elusive yellow ore, and, as Ridges later related, "it was not long before I found out what a Mormon was and I became one of them joyfully." Ridges subsequently moved to Sydney, where in November 1853 he and his wife were baptized into the faith of the Latter-day Saints by Elder Augustus Farnham. Having apparently profited from his foray into the gold fields, he "picked up" a two-storey house. There, relying on his woodworking skills and his recollections of the London organ factory, he began building his first organ.

His efforts were successful. The small instrument made a strong impression on his neighbors, who were also immigrants and had not heard an organ since leaving their homeland. It also impressed the presiding elder of The Church of Jesus Christ of Latter-day Saints, who suggested that Ridges donate the organ to the Church's headquarters in faraway Utah. Thus it was that in May 1856 the Ridges family, accompanied by some Mormon elders and the dismantled organ (soldered up in watertight metal cases), sailed for San Pedro, California, on the schooner *Jenny Lind*.[8]

Ridges and his family spent the following year in California, where he worked as a carpenter. But one of the Australian elders continued on to Salt Lake City and informed President Brigham Young of the organ they had brought. The following spring, a sizable wagon train left San Bernardino, bound for Utah. Among its passengers were Ridges and his family, and among its cargo was the organ. On June 12, 1857, "a very warm day," it was recorded that "a seven stop organ arrived from San Bernardino. This organ was donated by the Australian saints to the church and left at San Bernardino by the company of saints who brought it from Australia."[9]

Ridges set up the instrument in the old adobe Tabernacle, where it was used for the first time on a rainy Sunday, October 11, 1857.[10] The following spring it was hastily dismantled and briefly sent south with the choir and instrumentalists when Salt Lake City was threatened by Johnston's Army.[11] When it was returned, it seems to have been moved many times within the Old Tabernacle. After this building was razed in 1877, parts of Ridges's organ were used to build a larger instrument for the new Assembly Hall, which was completed on the same site in 1880.[12] Among the early organists who played the organ in the Old Tabernacle was Fannie Young Thatcher, a daughter of Brigham Young.

No stoplist of this organ has been discovered, and even its number of stops is uncertain. The account of its arrival in Salt Lake City mentions seven stops, and Ridges himself gave two differing accounts in later years. In one account he described it as an "organ with six stops,"[13] but in another interview, given a month earlier, he stated that "when finished the organ had about five stops outside of two mechanical stops, and perhaps 295 pipes."[14] Assuming that Ridges used the same 56-note manual compass that he later employed in his larger Tabernacle organ, this number of pipes could suggest five manual stops of full compass (280 pipes), possibly with a 17-note pedal stop (a total of 297 pipes). The seven stops mentioned in the account of the organ's arrival from California may thus have included the two mechanical stops mentioned by Ridges. With this small and much-traveled instrument began the history of the organ in Utah.

NOTES

1. John Longhurst, "The Salt Lake Mormon Tabernacle Choir." *The American Organist*, Vol. 22, No. 12 (1988).

2. Levi Edgar Young, *The Mormon Tabernacle with Its World-famed Organ and Choir* (Salt Lake City, 1930).

3. Jay M. Todd, "Tabernacle Organ." *Improvement Era*, Vol. 70 (Apr. 1967).

4. Graeme Rushworth, "An Organ for the Tabernacle." *The Tracker*, Vol. 24, No. 4 (1980).

5. Family History Library film #917111.

6. "Pioneer Organ Builder's Story," *Deseret News*, Feb. 16, 1901.

7. Civil Registration Marriage Certificate (St. Catherine's House, London).

8. Adelaide Whitely Ridges, ms. Autobiography (Church Archives).

9. *Journal History*, June 12, 1857.

10. *Journal History*, Oct. 11, 1857.

11. *Journal History*, Apr. 4, 1858.

12. *Journal History*, Aug. 17, 1907.

13. *Deseret News*, Feb. 16, 1901.

14. *Salt Lake Herald*, Jan. 2, 1901.

Joseph J. Daynes

The "Pioneer" Organ of Joseph Ridges and Niels Johnson

I am very proud of that organ, as proud as the proudest father could be of a distinguished son, and I have the satisfaction of knowing that when I am laid away to rest that organ will continue to stand as a memorial of the trials and difficulties that were overcome by the pioneers, breathing out strains of sweet music to delight future generations.[1]

JOSEPH H. RIDGES

About a year after their arrival in Utah, Joseph and Adelaide Ridges moved south to the settlement in Provo. There Joseph became a farmer and, in 1858 and 1860, took two additional wives. Meanwhile, in Salt Lake City, plans were being made for a newer and much larger Tabernacle that would accommodate the rapidly growing number of Latter-day Saints that continued to emigrate from many parts of the world. Even the earliest plans for this new Tabernacle assumed that it would have a large organ. Ridges recalled that Brigham Young, the leader of the Church and community, had said "that the Tabernacle must have a big organ which would be commensurate with the beauty and vastness of the building."[2] Young's plan was enthusiastically endorsed by other community leaders, and some time after 1861 Young sent for Ridges and asked whether he thought it would be possible to build such an organ in Utah. "I told him that I thought it could be done," Ridges reported.

By 1863 work on the new Tabernacle had begun. William H. Folsom had been chosen as the architect in 1861, and he was soon joined by Henry Grow, a bridge builder from Pennsylvania, who was responsible for the unique construction of the building's huge roof, supported only by the forty-four sandstone piers that ring the unusual ovate structure. Grow had built a bridge over Utah's Jordan River "after the Remington patent of lattice bridges, in which planking and pegs were used."[3] He proposed to adapt this technique to the construction of the Tabernacle roof, creating one of the major engineering feats of the nineteenth century.

Ridges too was busy with his commission. There was much preparation to be done, and in the office of Truman O. Angell, another architect involved with the Tabernacle project, he began making preliminary drawings. He must have realized very early that certain components, particularly metal pipes, would have to be obtained ready-made. Possibly he also realized that he had been essentially out of touch with developments in the organ-building trade since leaving London in 1851. Thus he set out for Boston, then a major center of organ-building, in the spring of 1863. Since the railroad did not come to Utah until 1869, Ridges traveled overland by stage to Omaha and proceeded from there to Boston by rail via New York.[4] Arriving on the 24th of June, Ridges lost no time contacting William B. D. Simmons, one of Boston's leading organ builders, and reported his activities in a letter to Brigham Young (original spelling and punctuation are retained in this and all succeeding quotations and stoplists):

During the past two days I have been busily engaged in geting my object underway. I am happy to say it is favourable progressing, the making [of] the metal pipes will detain me here five weeks unavoidably. The price of metal is a little higher than I expected, though not much, making perhaps in all my bills $100 more than the sum named by you to Bro. Eldridge. This class of goods has raised on account of the war and it is thought by the Builders will raise much more. Mr. B. D. Simmonds is considered to be the best Organ Builder here. With him I am dealing. He says the price of your organ if built at his Factory would be forty five Thousand Dollars.[5]

Confirmation of Ridges's visit to Boston and its mission is found in a brief notice that appeared a few months later in a Boston musical magazine, under the heading "A Large Organ in Utah":

> A large organ, one of the largest in this country, has recently been built by Simmons & Co. to be placed in the Mormon Tabernacle in Salt Lake City, which is a building large enough to seat 15,000 people. The case of the organ and the large diapasons, are to be made in the temple [sic: actually Tabernacle], and a skilful workman has started for this purpose to Salt Lake City.[6]

This notice appeared on September 5, 1863, and the "skilful workman" was probably Ridges himself. According to the bill of lading preserved in the Church Archives, Simmons had shipped six boxes of organ parts to Salt Lake City on August 13, so Ridges presumably left Boston at about the same time. The size of both the Tabernacle (which is said to have seated 5,000 to 6,000 people before the gallery was added) and the organ (initially a medium-sized, two-manual instrument) seems to have been exaggerated, but perhaps editor John S. Dwight was a bit carried away by the description of the 32' "large diapasons."

Just how much of the organ Simmons made beyond the metal pipes is open to some conjecture. While Ridges specifically mentioned metal pipes in his letter of 1863, in his 1901 recollections he itemized his Boston purchases

only as "spring wire, thin sheet brass, soft fluff leather to make the valves, ivory for the keys, and other things we could not make here."[7]

To complicate matters further, the bill of lading for the six crates that arrived shortly after Ridges's return listed the contents simply as "One Church Organ," although it also listed "2 small boxes . . . 16 inches long or 5 inches square," which may have contained the ivory, wire, brass, and leather mentioned by Ridges.[8]

Some time after William B. D. Simmons's death in 1876, a friend of his, the organ builder George S. Hutchings, said that Simmons had "built the action and complicated parts of the interior and did the voicing while the Mormons built the lower bass notes and the case."[9] However, Ridges on several occasions claimed to have done the voicing himself and in any event would have voiced his own wood pipes and regulated Simmons's metal pipes even if the latter had arrived prevoiced. A plausible scenario is that Simmons supplied a complete internal chassis for the organ—frame, windchests, key and stop action, and metal pipes—leaving the Pedal pipes and chests, the bellows, the case, and probably the manual wood pipes for Ridges and his crew to construct. Oral tradition indeed implies that Ridges made the smaller wood pipes in the manual divisions as well as the large Pedal pipes.

Of as much interest as what Ridges ordered while in Boston is what he saw there. Certainly he saw the interior of Simmons's large, up-to-date, steam-powered factory on the corner of Charles and Cambridge Streets in Boston's west end. And while waiting for Simmons to complete the ordered parts, Ridges may well have indulged his boyhood penchant for visiting churches to examine the organs within.

There were many churches within easy walking distance of Simmons's factory, most of them containing recently built examples of the Boston builders' art.

Also nearby was Boston Music Hall, only a few blocks' walk down Tremont Street from Seaver Place, from which Ridges addressed his letter to Brigham Young. In March 1863, after many delays, the internal parts of a large organ built by the Walcker firm of Ludwigsburg, Germany, had arrived at the Music Hall and were being set up during the summer months. The elaborate casework, designed by the noted Boston architect Hammatt Billings and made of solid black walnut by the Herter Brothers of New York, had already been completed, and it lay in pieces around the hall.[10] Although the Music Hall was closed while the "Great Organ" was being assembled, there is ample evidence that interested visitors were admitted during this period, including some of Boston's organists and organ builders.

It is hard to think that Ridges would not have taken the opportunity to study such an important instrument, and circumstantial evidence suggests that he did so. The casework he designed when he returned to Utah so closely resembles that of the Boston organ in both layout and detail that the similarity cannot be attributed to mere chance. The greatest similarity in the two designs is in the upper case. In contrast, Ridges's lower case was quite simple and much different than the lower case of the Boston organ. This would seem to suggest either that Ridges had a photographic memory, or, more likely, that he had seen drawings of the case or had made detailed sketches of the upper case parts while they were still laid out on the floor of the Music Hall.

Joseph Ridges and the organ parts from Boston arrived back in Salt Lake City in the fall of 1863. By this time the timber was being cut and the stone quarried for the new Tabernacle, but actual construction did not begin until September 1865.[11] During the interim, Ridges presumably occupied himself with designing the organ and procuring other materials.

Ridges needed clear, vertical-grain pine for the largest wood pipes, and Robert Gardner and his son William were given the task of finding it. According to family and local tradition, this choice material was finally located in Pine Valley, about 325 miles south of Salt Lake City.[12] The elaborate casework is also of pine, although skillfully grained to resemble oak. This pine came from a canyon near Salt Lake City, but Indians had driven off the settlers who were operating the sawmill there, and Ridges recalled that he and his helpers were "scared out of ten years' growth" by the unfriendly natives before getting their load of lumber safely back to their workshop. Glue and leather were other needs that could be met locally. Cow hides were chopped up and boiled down for glue in "big iron pots" outside the Tabernacle walls, and calfskins were used to hinge the ribs of the bellows and feeders.[13]

Ridges had found in the community "a few intelligent and skillful mechanics" to work with him, including Niels Johnson, Shure Olsen, David Anderson, William Pinney, and John Sandberg. None had ever worked at organ building before, so all had to be trained by Ridges, although toward the end of his labors he was joined by Frank Woods, presumably a recent arrival, who had worked in the organ building trade in England. Construction of the organ began in January 1866, and in May a newspaper reporter visited the workshop, observed the work in progress, and obtained the following description of the organ:

It has two manuals, or keyboards, and 27 pedals [keys], with a pedal compass of four C's to D. Its compass embraces 35 stops, five of which are mechanical. It will contain something like 2000 pipes, the largest one—CCCC—being 32 ft. in length. The two manuals are the swell organ and the great organ the stops of which, when played singly, produce the richest tones that modern art in organ building has produced, and when they are combined the volume of musical sound is grandly majestic. The instrument, when completed, will be 20 x 30 ft. and 40 ft. high and the cost of it, if made in the east and freighted here, would be over $30,000.[14]

By October 6, Ridges reported that the organ was partly set up "and gave us its opening tune this morning from seven hundred mouths"—or about twelve stops.[15] But apparently the organ was not yet in its permanent position, nor were the case and the large pipes finished. Quite possibly all that had been done at this point was to set up and adjust the chassis that had come from Boston. In this same account, Ridges recorded the stoplist of the organ for the first time (the stops rearranged in proper order; pitches added):

GREAT (56 notes)	SWELL (56 notes)
Bourdon [16']	Bourdon [16']
Open Diapason [8']	Open Diapason [8']
Stop Diapason [8']	Stop'd Diapason [8']
Hohl Flute [8']	Claribella [8']
Flute a Cheminee [8']	Principal [4']
Dulciana [8']	Clari. Flute [4']
Principal [4']	Stop'd Flute [4']
Flute Harmonic [4']	Piccolo [2']
Twelfth [2 2/3']	Mixture [2 ranks]
Fifteenth [2']	Cromorne [8']
Mixture [3 ranks]	Hautboy [8'; treble]
Trumpet [8']	Bassoon [8'; bass]

PEDAL
(27 notes)

Open Bass 32'
Open Bass 16'
Dul. Bass 16'
Stop'd Bass 16'
Principal Bass 8'

Ridges also noted that there were three couplers, but "composition pedals not yet

desided." This same stoplist, with even the same erratic order of the stops, appeared in the newspaper a year later with a few minute differences: the number of ranks in the Swell Mixture, omitted from Ridges's account, was cited, and the 32' Pedal stop was called "Great Open Bass." The couplers were identified as the usual Great to Pedal, Swell to Pedal, and Swell to Great, and a Tremulant and Bellows Signal were added to the mechanical stops.[16]

On August 6, 1867, Truman O. Angell, designer of the Tabernacle's interior, had overseen the placing of the stone foundations on which the supporting timbers for the organ would rest.[17] A few weeks later the newspaper reported that "the elevated part of the floor at the west end of the house was making rapid progress towards completion. Parts of the new organ were being placed back of it for putting up."[18]

The new Tabernacle was first used for a general conference on October 6, 1867. On this occasion, President Brigham Young

> thought it proper to say something of the unfinished condition of the organ. Not over one-third of the pipes were up, and till the casing was built, they had thrown around it a loose garment. It was now only about fifteen feet high, but when completed it would be forty feet high. Brother Ridges, and those who had labored with him, had done the best they could, and notwithstanding their diligence by early day, noon, and night, they had been unable to have it properly tuned. It was, however, in a condition to accompany the choir, and he was pleased with it.[19]

This account confirms that the organ case and large Pedal pipes had not yet been completed, but Ridges and his crew now concentrated all their efforts on the imposing case, and it was reported in May 1868 that Ridges had made a final design:

> The design is a very handsome one; and the front will be formed with flutings, panels, and pillars in the Corinthian style, tastefully carved and crowned with pyramidal tops. As the whole will rise over forty feet above the floor, the front, when completed, will present a massive and imposing

appearance, while there will be ample space for the display of artistic ability in elaborating the design.[20]

The "iron horse" came to Salt Lake City in January 1870, and the Tabernacle organ, although still incomplete, quickly became an attraction for travelers who walked the few blocks from the new railroad station to Temple Square to view it. Ridges, in his autobiographical notes of 1901, mentioned visits from such disparate groups as a dozen Washington congressmen and a delegation from Henry Ward Beecher's Plymouth Church in Brooklyn, New York. Invariably these visitors marveled at the 32' front pipes and expressed amazement that such a wonder could be a product of the "wild west."

By July 1869, the scaffolding had been removed and the organ case, with its decorations by pioneer wood carver Ralph Ramsey, had been grained and varnished to its present "faux oak" appearance. Since pine was the main source of timber for cabinetry as well as construction in the Salt Lake Valley, the early Mormons became impressively adept at wood-graining. Oak finish was popular, and fine examples are found in the Tabernacle and the 1880 Assembly Hall. In other pioneer buildings, such as the Lion House and Brigham Young's Beehive House, one also finds mahogany-grained doors and marble-grained mantels—all, like the Tabernacle's "marble" pillars, of native pine.

The newspaper account that reported the removal of the scaffolding from the case also recorded what remained to be done:

> Bro. Ridges informs us that a large amount of work has yet to be bestowed upon it and that the octave of immense pipes in front, which are now white, will be covered with gold leaf, and that many other smaller ornamental pipes have to be placed where the green drapery is now arranged, together with some beautifully carved panel work for the pedestal portion of the case.[21]

The reference to "carved panel work" is curious. The lower part of the case, now partly obscured, is indeed paneled but includes no carvings. Perhaps carved decorations for the lower case were originally planned but were not made due to cost.

The construction of the ten (not a full octave) largest display pipes has always been a matter of interest. The longest is 32 feet in speaking length (mouth to top), and all ten are made of pine, assembled in barrel-stave fashion. According to Ridges, the pieces were carefully fitted and glued, then "lashed together with rawhide thongs and strings of half-tanned calfskin."[22] This lashing would shrink as it dried, acting as a clamp to keep the joints tight while the glue set. The white finish of the pipes could be accounted for by what appears to be a coat of gesso or plaster of Paris still to be observed on the unfinished backs of the pipes. The late Alexander Schreiner, however, claimed that the front pipes were originally gold-painted and were not gold-leafed until around 1950. Current organ technician Robert Poll provides this observation about the construction of the wooden front pipes:

> The most interesting thing . . . is the construction method apparent from the inside. Except for a strip about 3 3/4" wide which runs the entire length of the resonator, the entire inside of the pipe has been smoothed with some kind of a scalloping tool in such a way that it was obviously done after the pipe was assembled. I conjecture the pipes were glued together with the glue absent only from the unfinished strip which was then removed when the glue had dried. A craftsman could then reach through this "slot" with a tool and smooth the interior after which the strip was glued back into the slot, the exterior smoothed and plastered.[23]

The actual reason for making the ten largest pipes of wood instead of tin or zinc was probably a simple matter of necessity being the mother of invention. Large metal pipes are costly and relatively fragile. Hence, transporting them overland to Utah before the advent of the railroad would have been virtually impossible. How Ridges chose his method of construction is another matter. The pillars supporting the gallery in the Tabernacle are of the same type of "barrel-stave" construction. But the gallery was a later addition, not begun until the fall of 1869,[24] and Ridges's wooden front pipes were already in the organ by this time.

The concept of making round wooden structures in this manner was not particularly unusual. A large organ built by the German firm of Walcker in 1856 for the Cathedral of Ulm, unfortunately no longer extant, had "a set of cylindrical wood 32 ft. pipes . . . plated with tin." These were situated in the case front, but it is not known how they were constructed.[25] Assuming that Ridges had contact with Walcker's workmen who were installing the organ in the Boston Music Hall in 1863, they may have suggested the idea to him. It is just as possible, however, that Ridges conceived the idea independently.

In the fall of 1869, Ridges made a second trip to Boston, this time by rail via Philadelphia and New York. His purpose seems to have been to purchase pipework and other materials for a third manual division—the Choir—again from W. B. D. Simmons. He spent part of his time looking at some of the newer organs in the city, including the completed Music Hall organ. As before, he reported his progress in a letter to Brigham Young, dated October 27:

> I have obtain admitance inside the organs I desired to see, and think I have seen none so grand as our own, with the third manual or key board and solo stops for concert and religious use it will compare with any.
>
> The exterior pipes in the Great Boston Organ are not so large as those in ours and altogether it is less grand than I had anticipated. As I write I am surrounded by seven fine church Organs in the

> Factory of W. B. D. Simmons who undertook my order lower than others so I delt with him. . . .
>
> I have only bought what I am obliged to have in order to make a fair finish of the Organ. I want two more stops—mettal to go with my wood stops but I feared you would not approve.[26]

Ridges's assertion about the pipes of the "Great Boston Organ" is correct. According to Robert Reich of the Andover Organ Company, curators of the instrument in its present home in Methuen, Massachusetts, the lowest front pipe is F, five notes above the low C of the Tabernacle organ. Ridges's last statement is a little ambiguous, as the Choir division did contain both wood and metal stops, although the reference to "my wood stops" might suggest that he was referring to the expansion of the Pedal division—perhaps by the addition of low-pitched (and therefore costly) reed stops. Such stops were later added by Niels Johnson.

Sixteen-year-old Joseph J. Daynes, like Ridges a native of England, had been appointed Tabernacle organist in 1867, and the organ seems to have been in fairly regular use from that time, even though work on it continued. George H. Careless began his long tenure as director of the Tabernacle Choir in 1864, and an early account of the use of the organ is recorded in a report of one of the semiannual Church conferences, held around 1870:

> The singing during the Conference has elicited general and well-merited praise and commendations. . . . The accompaniment on the large organ by young Brother Daynes showed that the young man is doing well, and he should feel encouraged to persevere diligently to attain excellence in his profession. Music is destined to reach a high degree of perfection among the Latter-day Saints.[27]

Ridges and two other men were still working on the organ at the end of 1874, when he responded to a request for a progress report from the presiding authorities of the Church in a letter dated December 2:

The Organ is nearly completed, but is at present partly dismembered in order to complete the connection of the large front Pipes, which cannot be done to advantage while the instrument is in use.

The number of men working on it is Three, including myself.

On the completion of the work on which the men I have, are mainly engaged—an item which the President on his departure requested me to have done—which will take about four weeks—tis intended to reduce the number of men to Two in all.

In Building a Grand Organ, on so great scale as ours, other Builders have ranks of workmen acquainted with its complicated action and vast Breathing Reservoirs—better perhaps than themselves, with us: it has not been so, I have had no such efficient aid, the more profound of the work, devolving upon myself. And when its—Three Thousand-Tongues are all under control, each must receive its final equipoise of voice and Tone—the most important and last of the work, and is called in Organ phraseology—Regulating. This I have yet to do.

I am therefore thankful to say that A short time will successfully complete the work.[28]

This is a significant reference to Ridges's involvement in voicing and regulating, and is of interest in that it suggests that although Simmons made the metal pipes, Ridges himself may indeed have made all the wood ones, including those in the manual divisions, four sets of which still exist. Recalling the early days of the choir and organ, choir director George Careless related the following account:

> When Joseph H. Ridges and his men were making the wooden pipes, they always submitted them to me to decide on the quality of the tones. When the voicing was satisfactory, the pipes were completed and put in place.[29]

The men still working with Ridges were probably Niels Johnson and Shure Olsen. That they had learned their lessons well is attested to by the fact that these two men were engaged to build an organ for the new Assembly Hall in 1878. Parts of Ridges's old one-manual organ brought from Australia were used, but a photograph of the instrument shows a good-sized two-manual organ with an impressive Victorian case. A newspaper article from the period confirms that "as it [the old organ] is being enlarged, with additional pipes, bellows, stops, etc., it can really be called a new organ."[30]

Both Johnson and Olsen were Scandinavians. Johnson was born in 1837 in Lund, Sweden, came to Salt Lake City in 1861, and died there in 1886.[31] Olsen, born in 1818 on the island of Skudness in Norway, arrived in Salt Lake City in 1849 via Illinois. He was a carpenter and musician and held several positions of responsibility in the Mormon Church before his death in 1901.[32]

At about the same time that Johnson and Olsen were building the Assembly Hall organ, Ridges seems to have left the Tabernacle organ project for other pursuits. Perhaps his reasons were economic; by the 1870s he had at least four wives and a number of offspring, and there must have been a good market for a gifted architect and builder in the growing city. Among the buildings he is known to have been responsible for are the Gardo House and Academy, Amelia Palace, Hammond Hall, and a Jewish synagogue.[33] But possibly he was simply needed elsewhere by the Church, for he is also said to have built a staircase in the Salt Lake Temple, which was still under construction and was not completed until 1893.

Then too, perhaps the death in August 1877 of President Brigham Young may have temporarily halted work on the organ, later described as still being in an "unfinished state" in 1878.[34] From the beginning Young had been a strong supporter of Ridges and his work, as suggested by an anecdote later told by George Careless. Careless had submitted to Young a seating plan for the choir, arranging the singers in rows in

11

front of the organ. Brigham Young responded, "Brother George, your plan is very good, but I will have to get you to alter it, as I am very proud of the organ, and do not want any singers in front of it, as they would hide the lower part of the instrument."[35]

The last work recorded as having been done on the organ for several years occurred in the summer of 1878. At this time the pitch of the entire organ had to be sharpened a half-step to make it usable with an orchestra—a process that took ten days and resulted in the shortening of most of the pipes.[36]

Some time after the Assembly Hall organ was completed, Niels Johnson was commissioned to enlarge the Tabernacle organ, adding a fourth manual division and enlarging the Pedal. In August 1883, ten crates of "Organ Ware" weighing almost 6,000 pounds arrived via the Utah Central Railway.[37] The *Deseret News* reported:

> The grand organ of the Tabernacle is about to be completed. Brother Henry Grow informs us that a heavy shipment of pipes and other apparatus has just been received for it from Steere and Farmer [recte: Turner], of Springfield, Mass. . . . Brother Grow purposes putting the newly arrived pipes and other articles in place without delay.[38]

An article the following day was more specific, noting that "nearly 1,200 pipes" would be added and that the tracker action would be replaced by a "pneumatic action."[39] This action was, as later accounts clearly show, a "helper" action of the "Barker machine" (pneumatic lever) type, used in large European organs since before the middle of the century, and in common use among the eastern American organ builders since the 1860s. The parts for this action presumably comprised the "other apparatus" ordered from Steere and Turner, along with the pipes for the new Solo division.

Johnson's work took two years, and when it was finished in the fall of 1885, a detailed account appeared in the newspaper. A brief history of the organ noted that the organ had been left in "an unfinished state" by Ridges and had subsequently been injured by incompetent tuners. Of significance, however, was the emphasis on keeping the organ up to date:

> Organ building has made immense progress during the last few years, and Mr. Johnson has introduced many of the best modern improvements.
>
> The interior of the organ is so arranged that all parts of the mechanism are easy to access.
>
> The pneumatic lever is applied to the great organ and its couplers rendering the touch—even with all the couplers on—as light as that of a piano.
>
> Another improvement is the putting in of a solo organ with six stops. This, together with the addition of other stops to the great, swell, choir, and pedal organs makes an addition of about 1300 new pipes.
>
> The organ has now four manuels and a pedal, the number of stops being 57. The total number of pipes is 2,648.
>
> The wind is supplied to the organ by three large bellows, which are operated by two hydraulic motors.
>
> The instrument has been almost entirely reconstructed in its interior parts; and in its now completed form it is justly an object of pride to every Latter-day Saint.[40]

The means by which the rebuilt organ was blown has been a matter of some conjecture. Ridges's original blowing mechanism was described as "four bellows," but what this probably means is either one large bellows with four feeders or two bellows with two feeders apiece—one for the manual divisions and one for the pedal division, which demanded considerable wind for its 32' stop and several 16' stops. Whatever the arrangement, the motive power was human, and several people still living in Salt Lake City recall ancestors who once served as Tabernacle organ blowers.

The 1885 account referred to the new blowing mechanism as "two hydraulic motors." This, along with some unsubstantiated oral tradition, led some later writers to assume that the bellows were actually operated by a water wheel run by a stream flowing under the Tabernacle. Although water from City Creek was apparently once diverted through the wall surrounding Temple Square, this predated the building of the Tabernacle and was done to supply water and power (by means of a large waterwheel) to the workshops located on the temple block in the 1850s. It may well be that recollections of this waterwheel later became the source of stories about powering the organ by similar means.

"Hydraulic motor" (or "water motor") was a common term for a device that was widely used from the 1870s through the early twentieth century for blowing organs in urban areas where relatively high mains pressure was available—especially since churches were not required to pay a water tax. These "motors" consisted of a reciprocating piston with two valves operating on mains pressure and connected in most cases directly to the blowing lever that operated the feeders. The fact that two hydraulic motors were used for the Tabernacle organ suggests that it had two sets of bellows in 1885, if not before. This would not be unusual for an organ of this size. Robert Poll notes that there are two bricked-up openings in a wall directly below the center of the organ, through which the mechanical linkages between the motors and the bellows may once have run.

Several firms in New England and New York manufactured hydraulic motors. Ross's and Whitney's were particularly popular with New England organ builders. Since Ross did not begin making water motors for organs until 1886, it is possible that the motors used in the Tabernacle, very likely sent with the other materials by Steere and Turner, were Whitney's "Improved Boston Water Motors." These had been in use since the 1870s and were noted for their durability and silence.[41]

Although a detailed description of the organ was promised in the 1885 article that announced its completion, the stoplist of the "Magnificent Instrument" was not printed until four years later:

GREAT (56 notes)	SWELL (56 notes)
Open Diapason 16'	Bourdon 16' (wood)
Open Diapason 8'	Open Diapason 8'
Viol D Gamber 8'	Salicional 8'
Hohl Flute 8' (wood)	Clarabella 8' (wood)
Stpt. Diapason 8' (wood)	Stpt. Diapason 8' (wood)
Flute a Chiminee 8'	Octave 4'
Octave 4'	Flauto Traverso 4' (wood)
Harmonic Flute 4'	Flutino 2'
Twelfth 2 2/3'	Dolce Cornet, 2 ranks
Fifteenth 2'	Cornopean 8'
Mixture, 4 ranks	Oboe & Bassoon 8'
Trumpet 8'	Vox Humana 8'

CHOIR (56 notes)	SOLO (56 notes)
Bell Gamba 8'	Stentorphon 8'
Gemshorn 8'	Keraulophon 8'
Dulciana 8'	Stpt. Diapason 8' (wood)
Melodia 8' (wood)	Harmonic Flute 4'
Lieblich Gedact 8' (wood)	Piccolo 2'
Fugara 4'	Tuba Mirabilis 8'
Piccolo 2'	
Clarionet 8'	
Fagotto 8'	

PEDALE
(30 notes)

Dbl. Op. Diap. 32' (wood)

Open Diapason 16' (wood)

Violone 16' (wood)

Bourdon 16' (wood)

PEDALE (cont.)

Violoncello 8'

Flute 8' (wood)

Trombone 16'

Trumpet 8'

COUPLERS	MECHANICALS
Great to Pneumatic	Swell Tremolo
Swell to Pneumatic	Pedal Check
Choir to Pneumatic	Wind Indicator
Solo to Choir	Hydraulic Engine Starter
Choir to Swell	Automatic Engine Regulator
Great to Pedale	
Swell to Pedale	
Choir to Pedale	

PEDAL MOVEMENTS

Great Forte

Great Mezzo, double acting

Great Piano, double acting

Swell Forte

Swell Piano, double acting

Pedal Forte

Pedal Piano, double acting

Balanced Swell Pedale[42]

Although only one 32' wood pedal stop is mentioned in this stoplist, it was not the original one. Ridges's impressive wooden façade pipes were now silent, having been supplanted by a new set of 32' open wood pipes of conventional square construction at the back of the organ. These pipes, unusual in that they have reversed upper lips, were presumably made by Niels Johnson and his workmen and are still in use in the present organ. Ridges's ten 32' pipes were to remain silent for nearly four decades. The reason for their abandonment can only be conjectured, but it very likely had something to do with the effects of varying humidity. Since the building was heated in the winter, dryness may have caused seams in the pipes to open up, adversely affecting speech.

A comparison of stoplists shows that other changes in Ridges's original work were minor, and the original windchests of the Great, Swell, and Choir were doubtless retained. The 16' Bourdon on the Great was replaced by a 16' Open Diapason, and in the Swell a Salicional was substituted for one of the 4' flutes and a Vox Humana added. No earlier stoplist for the Choir exists, but presumably this too was essentially unchanged. In the Pedal, aside from the substitution of the new 32' stop, the only changes were the addition of two reed stops and an 8' Flute. The Solo, of course, was entirely new, as was a portion of the action. And the console, still located below the central section of the case, must have been replaced or extensively rebuilt to accommodate the added manual, enlarged pedalboard, and new stops.

Although it would appear that demonstrations were played for tourists almost from the beginning, it is in connection with the enlarged organ that recitals are first mentioned. Thomas Radcliffe, a local musician described as "one of the best organists in the country," seems to have given a demonstration or recital for the Church members in October 1885, and some of the musicians in the city requested a public recital at a later date.[43] Certainly the Tabernacle now possessed an organ fully capable of recital work, but how much the organ was used for this purpose is not recorded.

In its final form, the original "pioneer" organ had a relatively short life. Tastes in organ tone were rapidly changing between 1885 and 1900, and much experimentation with new types of remote-controlled action was occurring in the same period. Until 1900 the Tabernacle organists had been relatively obscure individuals, probably all locally trained. But in October of that year, John J. McClellan, a musician of considerable training and stature, was appointed to the post. Although he was a Utah native, McClellan had studied at the University of Michigan and in Berlin.[44] He was conversant with the most recent trends in organ building and felt that the Tabernacle organ had fallen behind the times. Within a very short time he convinced the authorities that another rebuilding of the instrument was necessary, and a contract for this work was soon signed with the Kimball firm of Chicago.

On February 19, 1901, a testimonial benefit and concert was held in the Tabernacle for Joseph Ridges, whose recollections had been published in the *Deseret News* a few days earlier:

> On that occasion the grand old instrument as it came from the hands of the builder and as later improved by other artisans will be heard for the last time before again undergoing extensive improvements.[45]

This time, however, it was not a simple matter of completing work already planned or of making a few additions. Both the organ and the music program of the Tabernacle were to be quite radically transformed as the new century opened.

NOTES

1. "Pioneer Organ Builder's Story," *Deseret News*, Feb. 16, 1901.

2. Ibid.

3. Levi Edgar Young, *The Mormon Tabernacle with Its World-famed Organ and Choir* (Salt Lake City, 1930).

4. Jay M. Todd, "Tabernacle Organ." *Improvement Era*, Vol. 70 (Apr. 1967).

5. Letter from Joseph Ridges to Brigham Young. (Church Archives).

6. *Dwight's Journal of Music*, Vol. 23, No. 12 (Sept. 5, 1863).

7. *Deseret News*, op. cit.

8. Accounts and Invoices, extracted by Historical Department.

9. Christine Merrick Ayars, *Contributions to the Art of Music in America by the Music Industries of Boston* (New York, 1937).

10. *The Great Organ in the Boston Music Hall* (Boston, 1866).

11. Young, op. cit.

12. William J. Snow, "Robert Gardner." *Utah Historical Quarterly*, Vol. 9 (1941).

13. *The Great Mormon Tabernacle Organ* (Salt Lake City, n.d.).

14. *Deseret News*, May 24, 1866.

15. J. H. Ridges, ms. "Account of the Organ," Oct. 6, 1866 (Archives).

16. *Deseret News*, Oct. 9, 1867.

17. Truman O. Angell, ms. Personal Journal (Archives).

18. *Deseret News*, Aug. 21, 1867.

19. *Journal History*, Oct. 6, 1867.

20. *Deseret Evening News*, May 4, 1868.

21. *Deseret Evening News*, July 3, 1869.

22. *Journal History*, Aug. 1, 1901.

23. Letter from Robert Poll, Apr. 6, 1989.

24. *Journal History*, Aug. 21, 1869.

25. James I. Wedgwood, *Some Continental Organs and Their Makers* (London, 1910).

26. Letter from Joseph Ridges to Brigham Young (Church Archives).

27. Young, op. cit.

28. Letter from Joseph Ridges to Church Authorities (Church Archives).

29. Young, op. cit.

30. *Deseret News*, Nov. 27, 1878.

31. Obituary, *Deseret News*, June 2, 1886.

32. Obituary, *Journal History*, Jan. 8, 1901.

33. Graeme Rushworth, "An Organ for the Tabernacle, The Story of Joseph Harris Ridges." *The Tracker*, Vol. 24, No. 4 (1980).

34. *Journal History*, Oct. 3, 1885.

35. Young, op. cit.

36. *Deseret News*, Oct. 4, 1935.

37. Accounts and Invoices, op. cit.

38. *Deseret News*, Aug. 30, 1883.

39. *Deseret News*, Aug. 31, 1883.

40. *Journal History*, Oct. 3, 1885.

41. Laurence Elvin, *Organ Blowing, Its History and Development* (Swanpool, England, 1971).

42. *Deseret Evening News*, Mar. 2, 1889.

43. *Deseret News*, Oct. 3, 1885.

44. *The Diapason*, Vol. 16, No. 10 (Sept. 1925).

45. *Deseret News*, Feb. 16, 1901.

JOHN J. MCCLELLAN
AT THE KIMBALL CONSOLE, CIRCA 1910

The Kimball Organ

We feel that music-lovers will appreciate the fact that the new organ has tone qualities and shades not to be found in any other organ.[1]

FREDERICK W. HEDGELAND

John J. McClellan was appointed Tabernacle organist on October 1, 1900, and almost immediately he began to press for a major rebuilding and enlargement of the organ:

> He at once perceived the sore necessity of affecting some radical changes and improvements in the organ, in order to make it a modern instrument, and to relieve the player from the handicap under which he now performs, on account of the condition of the stops, etc.[2]

McClellan enlisted the support of the First Presidency and Bishop William B. Preston and likely convinced them that the work he had in mind could not be accomplished by the local artisans. At least two bids were received, one from Charles Klemt of Salt Lake City, presumably a local organ tuner who apparently planned to obtain some of the needed parts from Hook and Hastings of Boston. The other bid was from the Chicago firm of W. W. Kimball, one of whose representatives was invited to Salt Lake City to make an estimate. This was received on December 17, and two weeks later, on December 31—only three months after McClellan had begun his quarter-century tenure as organist—a contract was signed with Kimball for what would be essentially a new organ.[3]

Kimball was an interesting choice. William Wallace Kimball, an enterprising young man from Maine, began selling pianos and reed organs in Chicago in 1857. His success led to his opening a factory to make reed organs in 1880, and he expanded into piano manufacture in 1887. It was not until 1891 that the firm began building pipe organs, making it a relative newcomer to the field in 1900.[4]

Kimball was not an instrument maker but a businessman who hired capable people to run the various departments of his enterprise. Kimball's organ factory was headed by Frederick W. Hedgeland, a young scion of a respected English organ-building family who had emigrated to the Midwest a few years earlier. The first fruits of his association with Kimball were some ingeniously designed small "portable" organs, but within a few years Hedgeland was producing large instruments for prestigious churches and concert halls. All of these instruments employed a type of pneumatically controlled action for which Hedgeland received patents in 1892, 1896, and 1897.[5]

Only 2½ months after the contract was signed for the new Tabernacle organ, Hedgeland and a crew including Weiner, the firm's head voicer, arrived in Salt Lake City, along with a shipment of new pipework. The interior parts for the new organ had not yet arrived, but Hedgeland's men lost no time in removing the "pipes, windchests, and other portions of the organ." Soon the *Deseret News* reported:

> At the present time the grand old instrument presents a very forlorn aspect with the front [console?] torn out and the massive shell remain-

ing reared up towards the roof. All the choir seats situated immediately in the front of the instrument down to the rostrum have been removed, and the floor is being torn up. Already the curio and the relic hunters are beginning to flock to the scene to capture fragments of wood and metal that formed part of the grand old organ, which was commenced in the days before the whistle of the locomotive was heard in Utah.[6]

The new windchests, action, console, framework, and other parts—about thirty tons of material in all—arrived in early April via the Oregon Shortline Railroad. Shortly afterward, the railroad refunded the rather considerable freight charges, "to show appreciation for the many recitals and courtecies extended by the Church authorities in behalf of tourist[s] traveling over that line and passing through Salt Lake City."[7]

The contract had called for completion by April 1, but as the month neared its end the organ was still not finished. In response to complaints, Hedgeland blamed the delay on

the condition of the old work, which consists of the reinstallation of one-third of the old pipes, together with the entire pedal-chest and action. On getting into this work we found that it had suffered severely and that it required much overhauling in the way of renovation and repair in order that all the work should compare with the tone quality of the instrument.[8]

Hedgeland was consistently critical of the old organ. In all likelihood he would have preferred to have provided an entirely new organ, not using any portions of the old. As it was, the Kimball organ, although it utilized Ridges's casework and a few sets of old pipes, was in fact entirely new mechanically. It employed Hedgeland's patented "Kimball Duplex Pneumatic Action" (a form of tubular-pneumatic mechanism), which permitted the use of a detached console located directly in front of the choir director's podium, with the organist's back to the organ case.[9]

At least one person was concerned about the somewhat radical shift in the new organ's tonal emphasis. Professor Evan Stephens, the Tabernacle Choir's Welsh-born director, whose custom it was "to talk plainly to the members of the choir on matters musical," expressed to them his opinion that while he thought the new instrument "a fine organ, as pipe organs go generally," and comparable to large organs he had heard in London and Chicago, it nevertheless

entirely lacked the unique characteristics of the old instrument, which seemed almost human in its tone quality, while our present organ is decidedly instrumental. Many of the stops are quite characteristic of various instruments, but the organ lacks entirely the smooth, velvety pure tone quality that made our old organ different from any organ that I have ever heard. In times past I have gone away and have listened to the best organs that have ever been made, only to return here and enjoy the tones of the old instrument that much greater.[10]

Stephens, who incidentally here provides us with the only recorded description of the sound of the old pioneer organ, went on to say that he had once thought that the Tabernacle's unique acoustics were responsible for this sound. But then he realized that "the acoustic properties of the building simply reproduce the tone, good or bad, as it is given, and in as perfect a form as possible." Stephens was also concerned that the increased volume of the new organ would overwhelm the choir singers, who "might just as well stand still, wiggle their jaws and look as pleasant as possible."

Professor Stephens's criticisms quickly drew rebuttals from organist McClellan and builder Hedgeland. Calling the new organ "a grand, a matchless instrument," McClellan pointed out that the final voicing had not yet been completed, and that along with its increased volume, the new organ had "softer and more beautiful effects."[11] Hedgeland was far less diplomatic:

Ninety-six percent of the tone quality spoken of in the old organ was given it in the stock pipe shops in the East, or factories where these pipes are made, and where any one with the necessary means can buy them. They were voiced by very ordinary methods and were placed in the instrument without any further work being done on them, whereas, the stops in the present organ are built from scales, and voiced by men of world-wide reputation.[12]

While it is indeed true that the metal pipes, at least, were made in the East, they were hardly the work of "stock pipe shops." Both the Simmons and the Steere and Turner firms were highly respected organ builders in their day and were probably very careful to voice the pipes that had been ordered for an organ that had some renown even before its completion.

Hedgeland also brought in H. E. Freund, editor of the *New York Musical Age*, who seems to have been conveniently passing through. Freund backed up the builder by asserting that "the instrument is the finest I ever have had the pleasure of listening to."

The matter was finally laid to rest by a conciliatory editorial in the *Deseret News*. The editorial assured readers that the choir director and organist would work together to make certain that the organ did not overbalance the choir and that "in good time the choir, its leader, the congregation, and all listeners who come from afar, will be satisfied with the Tabernacle organ, and its fame will be increased instead of diminished by the work upon it which has been so long in contemplation."[13]

On May 4, 1901, the public had its first hearing of the completed organ in a recital by Dr. George W. Walter of Washington, D. C., consisting of four organ selections with a vocal solo, Mendelssohn's "Lord God of Abraham" (from *Elijah*), in the middle.[14] Two of the organ pieces were operatic transcriptions—the Overture to *Maritana* by William V. Wallace, and a "Mosaic Tannhauser" (presumably a medley) by

Richard Wagner. A third, "Vision in a Dream," was probably also transcribed, since its composer, a Danish writer of popular dance music and operettas named Lumbye, is not known to have written any organ works. The final selection was variations on "The Star-Spangled Banner," which may have been an improvisation, since Dr. Walter was noted as an improvisor.[15]

At about the same time, Thomas Radcliffe, a local organist who had once given a recital on the old organ, was requested by President Lorenzo Snow to give his opinion of the new one. Hedgeland showed Radcliffe and his son around the interior of the instrument, and Dr. Walter demonstrated the various stops. In a letter that appeared shortly afterward in the *Deseret News*, Radcliffe offered his impressions:

> I must confess that while listening to the recital yesterday, I thought there was not sufficient volume or breadth of tone (mind, I do not mean loudness or power), but rather, that glorious, full, round, rich diapason tone, which is the great charm of the organ, especially for church music and choir accompaniments, but after listening attentively, I have come to the conclusion that the volume of tone of those particular stops, is impeded by the very heavy case which incloses the instrument, I feel convinced that if some parts of it could be opened out, say the north and south sides, and some of the wood work in the front, it would make a great difference.
>
> I am very pleased with the string toned stops. I have never heard better, and can say the same of the reeds, and flutes.
>
> When inspecting the inside of the organ I took my son with me, who is a good practical mechanic, and he is very much pleased with the workmanship and does not think it could be better. I am also perfectly satisfied myself that the work is first class in every particular. I must congratulate you and your people in possessing such a magnificent instrument.[16]

The Kimball firm was quick to capitalize on the completion of an organ that it felt certain would enhance its reputation through its prestigious location. Just a month after the dedication concert, an article about it appeared in Kimball's own journal, *The Musical Herald*. Considering that a paragraph is devoted to disparaging the "old-fashioned" construction of the old organ, made "by the crude methods of hand labor, with comparatively little assistance from standard scales . . . and labor-saving machinery," it is likely that the article was written by Hedgeland. It goes on to state:

> Lately the instrument has been entirely rebuilt, revoiced, and brought not only "up to date" by the W. W. Kimball Company, but carried beyond, the expert of the house [Hedgeland?] having given rein to his imagination, and the result is an instrument which in size, quality and refined excellence must be one of the wonders of the organ-playing world.[17]

This was followed by an effusive tribute from Professor William P. Stewart of New York, who pronounced the organ "the latest round in the evolution of pipe instruments."

The original contract for the Kimball organ appears to have been lost, and no stoplist appeared in the newspapers. Fortunately, however, the Kimball console was preserved when the Austin organ was installed in 1916 and is now in storage at the Museum of Church History and Art adjacent to Temple Square. In addition, the Austin Organ Company recorded the stoplist in notes preserved in its files. Thus, although a few of the stopknob labels are now missing from the console, the original stoplist can be reconstructed from these two sources.

GREAT
(61 notes)

Double Open Diapason 16'

Bell Diapason 8'

Open Diapason 8'

Second Open Diapason 8'

Gamba 8' [tin]

Doppel Flute 8' [wood]

Dulciana 8'

SWELL
(61 notes, expressive)

Bourdon 16' [wood]

Horn Diapason 8'

Violin Diapason 8'

Stopped Diapason 8' [wood]

Spitz Flute 8'

Salicional 8' [tin]

Viole Celeste 8'

GREAT (cont.)

Claribell Flute 8' [wood]

Principal 4'

Wald Flute 4' [wood]

Twelfth 2 2/3'

Octave 4' [Austin: Fifteenth 2']

Trumpet 8' [Austin list only]

Cornopean 8'

Oboe d'Amour 8'

Vox Humana 8'

CHOIR
(61 notes, expressive)

Gross Gedeckt 16'

Geigen Principal 8'

Violoncello 8'

Quintadena 8'

Melodia 8'

Dolce 8'

Flauto Traverso 4'

Fugara 4'

Harmonic Piccolo 2'

Clarinet 8'

Orchestral Oboe 8'

PEDAL
(30 notes)

Double Open Diapason 32'

Open Diapason 16'

Bourdon 16'

Lieblich Gedeckt 16'

Violone 16'

Quinte 10 2/3'

Violoncello 8'

Flute 8' [wood]

Trombone 16'

Trumpet 8'

SWELL (cont.)

Aeoline 8'

Violina 4'

Flute Harmonic 4'

Flautino 2'

Cornet III

Contra Fagotto 16'

SOLO
(61 notes)

Violone 16'

Stentorphone 8'

Viole da Gamba 8' [tin]

Melophone 8' [wood]

Orchestral Flute 4' [wood]

Waldhorn 8' [Austin: 4']

Trumpet 8' [console only]

Tuba Mirabilis 8'

Saxophone 8'

Clarion 4'

PEDAL COUPLERS

Solo to Pedal

Swell to Pedal

Great to Pedal

Choir to Pedal

Pedal to Solo

Pedal Fifths

Pedal Octaves

SOLO COUPLERS

Solo to Great

So. to Gt. Super Octave

Solo Octaves

SWELL COUPLERS

Sw. to Gt. Sub Octave

Swell to Great

Swell to Great Super Octave

Swell Octaves

Swell to Solo

Swell to Choir

CHOIR COUPLERS

Ch. to Gt. Sub Octave

Choir Sub Octave

Choir to Great

ACCESSORIES:

Tremolos to Swell, Choir, and Solo

Reversible Gt. to Ped. [coupler]

Cresendo, Full Organ

Wind and Crescendo indicator dials

ADJUSTABLE COMBINATIONS:

3 Great, 3 Choir, 3 Swell, 2 Solo[18, 19]

The organ was blown by a 10 horsepower fan blower, and Austin lists the wind pressures as 4 1/4" for the Great and Solo and 3 1/2" for the Swell and Choir. The Pedal wind pressure is not given. All pipework not otherwise noted is presumed to be of spotted or common metal.

The number and extent of the couplers (note the "Pedal Fifths") were unusual for the day, particularly in organs that did not have electro-pneumatic action. The action that made them possible had only recently been patented by Hedgeland, and an account of his work states that in 1896 and 1897 "other remarkable patents were taken out for couplers for pneumatic action of this kind. By means of these patents they are able to make couplings to any extent required without impairing the prompt-ness of speech or the quality of touch of the keys."[20]

Unfortunately the preceding stoplist does not indicate how many stops were used from the former organ. At one point it was stated that "approximately one-third of the old pipes" were reused,[21] but Hedgeland was also quoted as saying that he had retained "only the pedal organ and a few stops" from the old instru-ment.[22] Comparing Kimball's Pedal division with that of the old organ that Johnson com-pleted confirms that the original eight stops were still present, with two more added.

Comments already quoted concerning the new "tone qualities and shades" (Hedgeland) and the "decidedly instrumental" character of the organ (Professor Stephens), along with Thomas Radcliffe's praise of the flutes, reeds, and strings (and disappointment with the diapa-sons), clearly indicate that the new organ was quite different tonally from the old. Although recitals are known to have been played on the old organ, no programs have survived. Dr. Walter's opening program on the Kimball organ, leaning heavily on orchestral transcrip-tions and improvisations, was fairly typical for the turn of the century, however, and the new organ was undoubtedly better suited to this type of literature than was the old.

After the opening of the Kimball organ, regular free recitals were scheduled on Wednesdays and Saturdays. The audience quickly grew to about 500 for the Saturday programs. In 1906 it was voted to continue the recitals on Tuesdays and Fridays.[23] By 1908 the popularity of the recitals had grown to the point that they were held every day except Sunday between the April and October general conferences of the Church.[24] A sampling of programs from this period, played by J. J. McClellan and, later, Tracy Y. Cannon and Edward P. Kimball, shows a balance between transcriptions and works written specifically for the organ. With the exception of an occasional large Bach work, the organ pieces were all written by late nineteenth- or early twentieth-century composers such as Guilmant, Batiste, Dubois, Gounod, Lefebure-Wely, Lemmens, Faulkes, Hollins, Kinder, Lemare, Harker, Malling, Gade, Elgar, and Rheinberger.[25]

During the fifteen years that the Kimball organ remained in use, the Tabernacle music program developed to something approaching its present form. The first assistant organist, Henry E. Giles, was hired in 1901. Although the Kimball firm was under contract to service the instrument annually for a few years, Giles also served as organ technician between these visits, earning a monthly salary of $25.00. He had been sent to Kimball's factory in Chicago to learn the intricacies of the organ's complex mechanism.[26] Edward P. Kimball and Tracy Y. Cannon—the latter a grandson of Brigham Young—were appointed assistant organists in 1905 and 1909 respectively.[27]

Another milestone of this period was the first of a long succession of commercial recordings by the Tabernacle Choir. This first recording was made in 1910 by the Columbia Phonograph Co., using the acoustical recording process.[28] Long before the choir's radio broadcasts began, these early recordings helped expand the musical fame of the Salt Lake City Tabernacle.

As late as 1912, the Kimball Company still boasted in *The Musical Herald* that its "noted organ," heard by "tourists from all parts of the world," was, thanks to Kimball technology, "up to the present standard of organ building."[29] But by 1914, heavy use and climatic conditions had long taken their toll on Hedgeland's complex tubular-pneumatic action. Originally designed for use in the small "portable" organs and later adapted for use in Kimball's larger instruments, this unique

mechanism eliminated the need of return springs in the pipe-valve pneumatics by using a two-pressure system, the two pressures deriving from a "bellows-within-a-bellows" wind system. The high pressure kept the square book pneumatics in the chest closed; the low (chest) pressure opened them. When adapted to large organs, this system had two basic weaknesses: its adjustment was critical and extremely sensitive to changes in humidity, and it was slow in its response.

In August 1914, organists McClellan and Cannon, with organ technician J. J. Toronto, brought the matter of the Tabernacle organ's condition to the attention of the First Presidency. They recommended that the organ be reconstructed by the Austin Organ Company of Hartford, Connecticut.[30] The matter—and the organ—lay dormant during the winter while other repairs were made to the Tabernacle interior.

This disuse exacerbated the mechanical problems of the Kimball organ. In March 1915, organist McClellan again pleaded his case for replacing the organ's mechanism. The pneumatics in the action were worn out, he said, but "even were they all replaced with new rubber the organ would still fail to respond to the touch of the player"[31]—an allusion to the slowness of response inherent in the two-pressure action even when it was in good condition. Organ technician Toronto corroborated his opinion, reporting that the organ "was beyond repair, and that its present collapsed condition had been hastened by the hardening of the rubber valves, caused by the heated condition of the building while undergoing its recent renovation."[32] The "rubber valves" were actually the chest pneumatics, which, like most of the other pneumatic work in the organ, were covered with flexible rubber-impregnated cloth. Hedgeland had found it necessary to use this impermeable material rather than the more traditional thin leather to avoid the slight leakage that would upset the critical balance of the two-pressure system. Unfortunately, this material was prone to stiffening when dried out and unused, and both of these conditions were present during the winter in which the Tabernacle was being renovated. The continued appeals of organists and technician did not fall upon deaf ears, and within the same month a contract for a new organ was signed with the Austin firm.

Shortly after the installation of the Kimball organ, Joseph Ridges had complained that Kimball, in its advertising matter, was taking all the credit for building the Tabernacle organ—and some of that credit did indeed still belong to him. When he passed away in March 1914 at age 87, he had come very close to outliving Kimball's work.[33]

NOTES

1. *Salt Lake City Tribune*, Apr. 19, 1901.

2. *Journal History*, Dec. 31, 1900.

3. Ibid.

4. Van Allen Bradley, *Music for the Millions: the Kimball Piano and Organ Story* (Chicago, 1957).

5. W. S. B. Mathews, "Mr. F. W. Hedgeland," *Music*, Vol. 16 (May 1899).

6. *Deseret News*, Mar. 15, 1901.

7. *Journal History*, Apr. 10, 1901.

8. *Journal History*, Apr. 20, 1901.

9. *Journal History*, Dec. 31, 1900.

10. *Salt Lake City Tribune*, Apr. 19, 1901.

11. *Deseret News*, Apr. 20, 1901.

12. *Salt Lake City Tribune*, op. cit.

13. "The Tabernacle Organ," *Deseret News*, Apr. 20, 1901.

14. *Journal History*, May 3, 1901.

15. Entry in *Baker's Biographical Dictionary of Musicians* (New York, 1940).

16. *Deseret News*, May 6, 1901.

17. "The Great Tabernacle Organ at Salt Lake City." *The Musical Herald* (May 1901).

18. Parley L. Belnap, "The History of the Salt Lake Tabernacle Organ" (diss., University of Colorado, 1974).

19. Tabernacle Organ file, Austin Organs, Inc.

20. Mathews, op. cit.

21. *Journal History*, Apr. 20, 1901.

22. *Journal History*, Mar. 15, 1901.

23. *Journal History*, Apr. 8, 1906.

24. *Journal History*, Nov. 14, 1915.

25. Tabernacle Organ Recitals file (Church Archives).

26. *Journal History*, Apr. 30, 1902.

27. Edgar V. Orth, "The Tabernacle Organ" (typescript).

28. Ibid.

29. "The 'Kimball' in Salt Lake City" *The Musical Herald* (Sept. 1912).

30. *Journal History*, Aug. 27, 1914.

31. *Deseret Evening News*, Mar. 17, 1915.

32. *Journal History*, Mar. 25, 1915.

33. *Deseret Evening News*, Mar. 9, 1914.

Frank W. Asper
at the First Austin Console, circa 1935

The Austin Organ *Opus 573, 1916*

*I have yet to hear its equal as to tonal quality,
abundance of color and general mechanical
accessibility and perfection.
It is a masterpiece and we are all proud of it
and grateful for its blessings to the
thousands of music lovers who flock daily to the
Tabernacle to hear its wonderful tones.*[1]

JOHN J. McCLELLAN

Although Professor McClellan and his assistants had proposed a new organ in the summer of 1914, repairs to the Tabernacle building took precedence. A new floor was laid, and all the pews were repaired and repainted. But during the winter that the Tabernacle was closed for repairs, the Kimball organ deteriorated further from dryness and disuse, becoming virtually unplayable. The Austin Organ Company had already submitted a proposal for a new and larger instrument, and on March 18, 1915, President Joseph F. Smith and Bishop C. W. Nibley signed a contract with that firm. The contract specified a four-manual organ with a "floating" String division and a Celestial division located at the opposite end of the vast room.[2]

The promised completion date was February 15, 1916, but meanwhile something had to be done to make the Kimball organ operable. The answer was to install a new console and bypass most of the old action:

> An entirely new console will be installed in the Tabernacle organ within the next six weeks according to a telegram received this morning by Presiding Bishop C. W. Nibley from the Austin Organ company of Hartford, Conn. The mechanism connecting the new console with the organ pipes will be electrical and will do away with the pneumatic tubes within the organ which have been causing the recent trouble with the instrument.
>
> The Austin company gives the assurance that the organ will be ready for use within the time specified so that the customary recitals for the summer will probably begin about the latter part of April.[3]

In addition to installing the console, Austin removed or bypassed the entire Kimball mechanism from console to windchests, substituting an electrical primary action for the pneumatic primaries. It would appear that the action of the Kimball had already been partially electrified, although no specific record of this work has been found. A letter from J. J. Toronto, written just before Austin's work was done, stated that "our present magnets have given more or less trouble for a long time and I believe if you can possibly do so it would be a very good thing to put in your own magnets for all the manuals, Pedal, and stop action etc."[4] Toronto's letter also suggests that the pipe-valve action had recently been releathered. Austin did not quite make the six-week deadline, but the new console and action were installed and in use by May 11, and the summer recitals went on as scheduled.[5]

It had been in 1899, just one year before the previous Tabernacle organ was built, that John T. Austin, like F. W. Hedgeland an English immigrant of a particularly inventive turn of mind, established a company in Hartford to build organs of a unique mechanical design. Unlike Hedgeland's action, which was very vulnerable to derangement because of its complexity and close tolerances, Austin's "Universal Airchest" and all-electric console were marvels of simplicity and ruggedness. And if something did go wrong, all the parts were accessible and standardized for easy replacement.

Soon after establishing his company, Austin began securing large contracts. In 1914 the firm had moved into a large new factory with its own power plant, two demonstration studios, and seven voicing rooms.[6] Austin had already built large four- and five-manual organs for such places as City Hall Auditorium in Portland, Maine; Medinah Temple in Chicago; and the Spreckles Open Air Auditorium in San Diego. In the year Austin signed the contract for the Tabernacle organ, the company was completing a 121-stop organ for the Panama Pacific Exposition Festival Hall in San Francisco, upon which J. J. McClellan gave one of the first recitals.[7] Nor was Austin unknown in Utah, for in 1907 the firm had built an organ of three manuals and 34 stops for the Mormon Tabernacle in Provo. Of four original bidders, the Provo organ committee narrowed the field down to two—Kimball and Austin—and eventually settled on Austin.[8] It is possible that Austin was the low bidder, but it is also possible that word had reached Provo Tabernacle organist C. W. Reid that the Salt Lake City Kimball was already having action problems. Conversely, it may have been because of satisfaction with the Provo instrument that Austin was chosen for the Salt Lake City commission.

During the summer of 1915, Toronto sent Austin detailed measurements of the organ case and floor area. Toronto also made a few suggestions based on his experience with the acoustical effect of the old instrument:

> [I] still think the organ would sound better if the topboards of the manual chests were 10 ft above the floor. According to your blue print the top boards are only 8 ft above the floor. Our present Gr[ea]t and Choir Organs are a little over 10 ft above floor. If you put them lower [I] am afraid the case will have some effect on the tone. There are no openings in case until about 11 ft above floor. Another thing I think would be an improvement. The Pedals which you show in your blue print on the outside of C side of Orchestral Organ could be put in the back as there would be room and the sound comes over nicely from the back.[9]

After the Tabernacle recital season ended in October, work on the organ began. Basil G. Austin, vice president of the Hartford firm and brother of its founder, stopped in Salt Lake City on his way back from the San Francisco Exposition. He was shown around by Toronto, who was already doing preparatory work:

> Mr. Austin expressed himself as pleased with conditions there, and thought that the organ would be rebuilt by the middle of February. He said Frank Steere, the building expert now finishing a job in Chicago, ought to be here any day, and expects the first shipment of pipes and material would be on hand by the coming week.[10]

Frank Steere (who, coincidentally, was the son of John W. Steere of the Steere and Turner firm, which had sold pipework to Niels Johnson in 1885) had previously checked out the Kimball for usable pipes with G. E. LaMarche of the Austin firm. Their comments show that some of the pipework was not in good condition. Many of the tuning ears of the Great Bell Diapason were broken off, and the Solo Clarion "hasn't been used for years." While they found much that was reusable, including a "well liked" Horn Diapason and several Pedal stops "in good shape," the Stentorphone was "very windy," and they had little good to say about the reed stops, which were generally noted with remarks such as "not good," "should be revoiced," or "not modern in design."[11]

Austin used more than half of the stops from the Kimball organ in the new instrument and claimed that "25 percent of the total number of pipes in the instrument are the original pipes placed in the organ when it was first built."[12]

26

But only one such stop can be positively documented with regard to its place in the original organ, although a few others are known to still exist, both in the Austin organ (now at Brigham Young University in Provo) and in the present Salt Lake City Tabernacle organ. In a letter to Herbert Brown of the Austin firm, written shortly after the signing of the contract, McClellan, Cannon, and Toronto made the following request:

> In the "Choir" of our present organ we have a delicious "Lieblich Gedeckt" 16', which is one of the original pipes built in 1860 by our revered Joseph Ridges, the Father of the organ, under Pres. Brigham Young.
>
> Can you not put this stop into the new choir, or have you arranged to use it elsewhere? It seems to us that the choir needs this character of stop.[13]

The stop in question was presumably the old 8' Lieblich Gedeckt of Ridges's 1869 Choir division, renamed Gross Gedeckt by Kimball. When it was moved to 16' pitch is a mystery, for with the exception of a newer low C put in to repitch the stop, the pipes of the bottom octave are not Kimball's. The Lieblich Gedeckt ended up in the Orchestral division of the new organ. It was also one of the few old stops to be retained in the present 1948 Æolian-Skinner organ, where it is now located in the Swell division, still at 16' pitch.

In the same letter was a request for more sub- and super-couplers and a 16' stop in the Celestial division. There was also a plea for retaining Kimball's Vox Humana, "the best voice stop we have ever heard," with the following rather extraordinary testimonial:

> Paderewski, Schumann-Heink, Patti, Eames, Nordica, Damrosch, Leoncavallo, Hegner, and others have told the organist that the Vox Humana is the greatest they have ever heard and this opinion is the generally accepted standing of the famous stop. The wave, decided and very human, or rather violin-like, of the tremolo (attached to the vox) is the most effective we know of.[14]

Brown replied that the console was almost finished, and therefore no additional couplers were possible, and that a 16' stop was unnecessary in the Celestial: "The sub couplers will do all this kind of work for you." But he promised to retain the Vox Humana "and in every way maintain the present wonderful effect of same."[15]

Austin's organ was larger than Kimball's in its number of stops. Unlike the previous organs, in which the manual divisions could be accommodated behind the original case by stacking them at different levels, the Austin organ was laid out with all divisions at the same level.[16] This was said to have been done to provide maximum stability of tuning, but it also helped to accommodate Austin's efficient but space-consuming "Universal Airchests," in which a person could stand upright. Because of this and the increased number of stops, it was necessary to extend the casework on both sides by fifteen feet. The architectural firm of Cannon and Fetzer was commissioned to design the new wings, with the understanding that the original case remain unaltered:

> In every detail of construction and decoration the additions to the organ will correspond with the original instrument, so the sense of at homeness of those who attend future organ recitals, concerts, and regular services in the tabernacle will not be lacking.[17]

The new sections echo the designs of the original case and are curved to follow the shape of the wall, the end towers being 24 feet high. Fetzer's cabinet shop showroom still proudly displays photographs of the organ case. The total dimensions of the enlarged case were 60 feet wide by 26 feet deep by 55 feet high.[18] Only one very minor change was made to the appearance of the old case. The line of the mouths in the central section of display pipes had originally been horizontal, like that of the central section in the Boston Music Hall case. But the center pipe in the case front was replaced, and the mouth of the new pipe is higher than its neighbors.

The additions to the case, which gave the organ the appearance it has today, were not the only changes made to accommodate the new instrument. The choir gallery stairways had to be remodeled, and at the opposite end of the auditorium, a basement room 25 by 20 by 16 feet in size was built to house the Celestial division:

> The echo [Celestial] organ is sunk under the floor at the east end of the tabernacle with its separate air chamber, and by a hood the sound will be deflected against the back interior wall throwing it out like a fan over the upper wall and ceiling, and spreading it out over the main interior.[19]

In any building but the Tabernacle such a placement would have been disastrous, but considering that building's unique acoustics, it was probably reasonably effective.

In a later account, organ technician Toronto noted that the pipes of this division were located six feet below the floor. Rather than having a separate blower, the wind for the Echo traveled 225 feet from the main blowers via a 10" conduit. Toronto also explained that "[the pipes] are connected on a duplex control basis, so that a melody and its accompaniment can be played on the [Celestial] organ."[20]

Wind for the organ, which used higher wind pressures than its predecessors, was supplied by two large Spencer centrifugal fan blowers located in the basement. A motor-driven 40-ampere generator supplied the action current. The compact new detached console was, unlike that of the Kimball organ, connected to the organ only by a flexible and detachable cable. Two junction boards in the floor allowed it to be moved to different locations on the rostrum.[21]

Frank Steere supervised the installation of the new organ during the winter of 1915-16, assisted by John J. Toronto.[22] The instrument was usable for the general conference in April and completed the following month. On May 12 a public concert was given which included choral and vocal selections. The organ pieces, played by John J. McClellan, included two transcriptions—Edward MacDowell's "To a Wild Rose" and selections from Pietro Mascagni's opera, *Cavalleria Rusticana*. Other organ pieces included Franz Liszt's Prelude and Fugue on B-A-C-H, J. S. Bach's Toccata and Fugue in D Minor, and an intermezzo by Callaerts. The closing piece was listed simply as "Annie Laurie"—probably an improvisation by the performer on the familiar tune.[23]

Despite the new instrument's unquestioned capability for rendering operatic excerpts, at least one knowledgeable individual in the musical community seems to have been unimpressed. In his memoirs, Alexander Schreiner recalled that "Emma Lucy Gates Bowen, our beloved and respected opera singer, said that in 1915 the new Austin organ did not please her as much as the one it replaced."[24] So the ill-fated Kimball organ was not entirely without its admirers.

Shortly after the organ was completed, the Austin firm published a handsome brochure describing the Tabernacle organ. Comparison of the stoplist with that published in the *Deseret News* on May 7, 1916, tallies in every respect but one: the old Lieblich Gedeckt was, probably accidentally, omitted from the Orchestral Organ in the newspaper version. Austin's 1915 tonal design was even more unabashedly "orchestral" than that of its Kimball predecessor, and in such a tonal scheme, along with consciously imitative flute and reed colors, string-toned stops played a prominent part:

In addition to the usual "string" stops found in the various departments of this organ, a special "String Organ" is also provided. This consists of seven ranks, or sets of specially scaled and voiced "string stops," accurately balanced and tuned in unison, sharp, and flat pitches, forming one magnificent string "Celeste." It is enclosed in a separate swell box and is playable from any manual at will.[25]

This division was located at the back of the organ, behind the swell boxes of the other divisions, but the curve of the Tabernacle ceiling probably distributed its sound quite effectively throughout the building.

The specifications for the organ had been drawn up by John J. McClellan, his assistants, and representatives of the Austin firm, including vice president Basil G. Austin. The latter expressed a common tonal philosophy of the period during his visit to Salt Lake City in 1915, when he stated that "the tendency now is to do away with 'mixtures,' as their 'screechy' characteristics make them undesirable, and they are easily replaced by other arrangements in pipe combination and construction."[26] The thinking of the times was that the extreme harmonic development of some of the keener-toned strings obviated the necessity for the "artificial" harmonics provided by the mixtures. This is nowhere better expressed than in a note in the Tabernacle contract under the Swell stoplist that reads, "If the Orchestral Celeste is drawn with the Viole d'Orchestre, it will make a wonderful 3 rank Mixture."[27] Indeed, the only actual mixture stop in the organ—the Swell Cornet Mixture—was itself made up of string pipes and was meant to add "shimmer" to the massed string stops rather than to reinforce the chorus.

A much more subjective idea of what was behind this and other "orchestral" tonal schemes is found in Austin's brochure describing the Tabernacle organ. Following references

to massive *crescendi* and *decrescendi*, "changing in color and warmth," we read:

> Now in the distance we hear a hundred violins and 'cellos in exquisite shimmering harmony, while silvery chimes ring out an angelus; liquid flutes and shepherds' pipes float all around us, and celestial harps are somewhere playing.
>
> A sonorous tuba now leads in a major theme, backed by the rich orchestral tones of clarinets, horns and strings; and then they sink and fade, while gradually arise diapasons, piling up in growing power with full-toned flutes; a glorious dignity of true organ tone triumphant.[28]

This excerpt does indeed describe one facet of the use of a large organ in a reverberant space, and an organist skilled in the style can create such moods with it. But when an organ is so exclusively oriented toward a single style of playing—as the 1915 organ unquestionably was—its deficiencies in the interpretation of other types of music eventually become evident.

In 1924 two young new organists, Alexander Schreiner and Frank W. Asper, were appointed to the Tabernacle, although senior organist McClellan and his two assistants, Kimball and Cannon, remained. The following summer, on July 3, John J. McClellan suffered a stroke as he was completing a noonday recital. "The last number on his program was Handel's Largo, and as he was playing it suddenly both of his hands fell on the keys."[29] He recovered sufficiently to resume teaching, but a second stroke, occurring a few weeks later during a lesson, proved fatal. His funeral was held in the Tabernacle, and prior to it Edward P. Kimball played a recital of pieces said to have been among Professor McClellan's favorites, including Handel's Largo, Lemare's Andantino, Schumann's "Traümerei," and Chopin's "Marche Funebre."

Gifted and well-educated (Schreiner was at the time of McClellan's death studying with Charles-Marie Widor at Fontainebleau), the two new organists were worthy inheritors of the deceased musician's mantle. As with many others of their generation, their concepts of organ design were more eclectic. In the fall of 1926 the first of several tonal changes in the 1915 organ were made by Austin. Sixteen new stops (4 Great, 3 Swell, 3 Orchestral, 2 Echo, 4 Pedal) were added, most of them 8' color stops. But in the Great, the Principal 4' and Fifteenth 2' were moved to the unenclosed portion and a 5-rank Mixture added, providing a complete diapason chorus heretofore lacking. The 3-rank Cornet in the Swell was replaced by a 4-rank Plein Jeu,[30] a stop that was revised again in 1933. In addition to these tonal changes, a new set of chimes was placed in the Great, all tremulants were replaced, and Joseph Ridges's front pipes, silent since 1885, were put on new action and reconnected to provide a 32' bass octave to the new 16' Major Diapason in the Pedal.[31]

A newspaper article that appeared at the time stated that "the instrument now possesses possibilities of quality and beauty of tone not before obtainable," noting also that "a number of the added stops are directly in front of the instrument and immediately behind the singers, giving invaluable support." But the changes also signalled a new way of thinking that was gaining ground in the organ world:

> Nothing of theatrical effect has been added to the great instrument, but everything is of real organ character approved by organ experts and artists, and now definite features of standard organ construction.[32]

According to Austin's brochure, more than 250,000 people heard the organ live each year during the daily recitals. Many more were soon to hear it, for on July 15, 1929, "Radio station KSL had to go off the air for a few minutes while its one and only microphone was carried from the station to the Tabernacle" for the first nationwide broadcast of the

Tabernacle choir and organ over the NBC network.[33] Three years later the Sunday morning program "Music and the Spoken Word" transferred to CBS. Until the advent of E. Power Biggs's radio program in 1937 (often heard back-to-back with the Tabernacle program until 1958), the Tabernacle broadcast was practically the only source of legitimate organ music on the airwaves.

Beginning with John J. McClellan, the twentieth-century Tabernacle organists were well known as recitalists. In addition to his duties at the Tabernacle, McClellan also directed the Salt Lake Opera Company and Salt Lake Symphony at various times. He also taught at Brigham Young University and the Utah Conservatory and somehow found time for occasional recital tours. His successors Asper and Schreiner were even more active in this area, touring regularly under professional management. These recital tours brought them into contact with some of the newest and best instruments in the country, which must have made them increasingly unhappy with the shortcomings of the 1915 Tabernacle organ.

With the daily recitals, Sunday broadcasts, rehearsals, conferences, and other functions, the organ was heavily used, and by 1937 it needed an overhaul. In February of that year the daily recitals, played throughout the year since 1925 and so popular "that the railroads have arranged their schedules so that passengers may attend," were suspended for a few weeks. During this time, Austin installed a new console (with many more couplers and combination pistons than the old one) as well as new relays, and replaced all the chest pneumatics.[34]

Three years later, Austin was again called in, this time to make more tonal changes. With the exception of a new Trompette 8' in the Swell and a Fugara 4' in the Orchestral, these consisted of adding mixtures and mutations to the Great, Swell, and Choir. James B. Jamison was responsible for the design of the new stops, including scaling and mixture composition. It was stated that the work was "intended to increase the color and brilliancy of the instrument." At the same time the existing reed stops were all revoiced by James H. Nuttall of California.[35]

The nature of these changes indicates the direction in which the Tabernacle organists were thinking. Jamison was one of the early standard-bearers of the "American Classic" movement as well as Austin's West Coast representative. He was also the author of a series of articles expounding current concepts of organ design, which appeared during 1939 and 1940 in *The Diapason*. Alexander Schreiner thought enough of these articles to write to the magazine and commend the editor for publishing them.[36]

Further tonal alterations were apparently planned for the Austin organ, but World War II intervened, temporarily halting all organ work because materials were unavailable. In his autobiography, Dr. Schreiner stated that by 1943 the need was felt for "a louder organ tone and a greater variety of tonal colors. This made it again necessary to plan a more highly developed instrument."[37] By this time the acknowledged leader of the "American Classic" movement was not Austin but the Boston firm of Æolian-Skinner. Although the correspondence begun in 1944 with that firm's tonal director, G. Donald Harrison, initially was directed toward a tonal revamping of the Austin, the actual result was an entirely new organ, completed in 1948. With the exception of a few stops retained for use in the new organ, the Austin organ was removed by the Schoenstein firm of San Francisco to the Auditorium of the Joseph Smith Building at

Brigham Young University in Provo, losing its String and Celestial divisions in the process, as well as the enclosed portion of the Great.[38] It was extensively rearranged and was installed in a chamber that had none of the acoustical advantage of the Tabernacle's open and reverberant space.

The original stoplist of the Austin organ, taken from Austin's brochure, is as follows. The stops marked with an asterisk [*] are identified in a shop copy of the contract as being reused from the former organ, and notes in brackets are from the same source:

GREAT ORGAN (61 notes)
5" wind; all but first six stops enclosed in Orchestral box
* Contra Bourdon 32' [from Pedal]
* Double Open Diapason 16' [32 from Pedal]
  Bourdon 16' [from Pedal]
  Flauto Major 8' [ext. Pedal Open]
* First Diapason 8' [40 scale]
* Second Diapason 8' [41 scale]
  Bell Diapason 8' [46 scale]
* Violoncello 8' [former Gamba; 53 scale]
* Doppel Flute 8' [6 x 5 1/2]
  Gedeckt 8' [from Bourdon]
* Clarabella 8' [6 x 5 1/2, open to CC]
* Wald Flute 4' [4 x 3]
* Principal 4' [56 scale]
* Fifteenth 2' [69 scale]
  Double Trumpet 16' [7 1/2", from Trumpet; new bass octave]
* Trumpet 8' [6"]
  Clarion 4' [from Trumpet; new treble octave]

SWELL ORGAN (61 notes)
5" wind
* Bourdon 16' [7 x 8]
  Diapason Phonon 8' [40 scale, wood bass]
* Horn Diapason 8' [43 scale]
* Gross Flute 8' [6 x 5, former Melophone, open to CC]
  Viole d'Orchestre 8'
  Orchestral Celeste 8' [2 ranks]
* Aeoline 8' [60 scale]

31

SWELL ORGAN (cont.)

* Aeoline Celeste 8' [56 scale, tenor C]

  Concert Flute 8'

  Unda Maris 8' ["to undulate with Concert Flute"]

* Flute Harmonic 4' [69 scale]

* Violina 4' [69 scale]

* Flautino 2' [74 scale]

* Cornet Mixture III [12, 15, 17; 1 1/2, 1 1/4, 1 1/8]

* Contra Fagotto 16' [5 1/2", 85 notes]

* Cornopean 8' [from Contra Fagotto]

* Oboe 8' [former Oboe d'Amore]

* Vox Humana 8' ["separate chest and Tremolo"]

  Tremulant

ORCHESTRAL ORGAN (61 notes)

5" wind; many stops from former Choir division

* Lieblich Gedeckt 16' [8 x 9; former Gross Gedeckt]

* Geigen Principal 8' [6 scale]

* Melodia 8' [6 x 5 1/2, open to CC]

  Orchestral Viole ["new Nitsua"]

  String Celeste II ["sharp rank Nitsua 73, flat rank Viole Cel. TC 61"]

* Dolce 8' [56 scale]

* Quintadena 8' [56 scale]

* Flute Octaviente 4' [3 x 3, wood; former Fl. Trav.]

* Piccolo Harmonic 2' [69 scale]

  Double Oboe Horn 16'

  Oboe Horn 8' [from Double O. H., prepared for]

* Clarinet 8' ["bell top"]

  Cor Anglais 8'

  Concert Harp [from Solo]

  Chimes [25 notes]

  Tremulant

SOLO ORGAN (61 notes)

10" wind

* Violone 16' ["about 41," former Contra Violone]

  Flauto Major 8' ["stop bass"]

* Stentorphone 8' [38 scale]

* Gross Gamba 8' [54 scale, tin; former Viole di Gamba]

* Gamba Celeste 8' [56 scale; former Sw. Salicional]

* Orchestral Flute 4' [4 1/2 x 4, former Doppel Flute]

  Tuba Profunda 16' [9"; from Tuba, new bass octave]

* Tuba Harmonic 8' [5"; former Tuba Mirabilis]

  Tuba Clarion 4' [from Tuba; new treble octave]

  Tuba Magna 8' [5"; 15" wind]

SOLO ORGAN (cont.)

  Concert Harp [bars and resonators; 61 notes]

  Chimes [from Orchestral; 25 notes]

  Tremulant

CELESTIAL ORGAN (61 notes)

5" wind; playable from both Great and Solo

  Cor de Nuit 8'

  Viole d'Orchestre 8'

  Viole Celeste 8' [73 scale]

  Viole Aetheria 8' [70 scale]

  Dolce Celeste 8' [70 scale; 61 notes from Tenor C]

* Gedeckt 8' [6 x 5 1/2; former Sw. Stopped Diapason]

  Fern Flute 4'

  Horn 8' [large, "small Har. Tuba voice smooth"]

  Vox Humana 8' ["separate chest and swell box"]

  Celestial Harp 8' [61 notes; "regular A O Co. Harp"]

  Tremulant

STRING ORGAN (61 notes)

A special separate STRING ORGAN of Seven Ranks of pipes of 8 feet pitch, composed of various scales and voicing, and tuned as a large magnificent Celeste.

  Two of the Ranks of normal pitch

  Three of the Ranks slightly sharp and

  Two of the Ranks slightly flat

This section is a separate division, enclosed in its own swell box, with four appropriate pistons for the purpose of switching same on to any desired manual at will.

The Swell Box will switch automatically on to the Swell Pedal belonging to the particular manual that the String Organ is switched on to.

PEDAL ORGAN (32 notes)

5" wind; augmented

  Gravissimo 64' (Resultant) [from 32' Diap. and 32' Bourdon]

* Double Diapason 32' [24 x 22; "lowered to Int. pitch by sliders"]

* Contra Bourdon 32' ["new 13 notes then old moved up one pipe"]

* First Diapason 16' [ext. 32' Diapason]

* Second Diapason 16' [from former Gt. metal Diapason]

  Violone 16' [from Solo]

* Bourdon 16' [9 1/2 x 9 o.d., from 32' Contra Bdn., "moved up one"]

PEDAL ORGAN (cont.)

* Dulciana 16' [former Gt. Dulciana with new bass octave]

  Lieblich Gedeckt 16' [from Swell]

  Sub Bass 16' [from Celestial]

  Quint 10 2/3' [from Bourdon]

  Gross Flute 8' [from Open Diapason]

  Flauto Dolce 8' [from Bourdon]

  Violoncello Celeste 8' [2rks, from Solo]

  Octave Flute 4' [from Open Diapason]

  Contra Bombarde 32' [from Solo Tuba Magna]

  Bombarde 16' [from Solo Tuba Magna]

  Tuba Profunda 8' [from Solo]

  Tuba Harmonic 8' [from Solo]

  Tuba Clarion 4' [from Solo]

  Fagotto 16' [from Swell]

COUPLERS

  Solo to Pedal 8', 4'

  Swell to Pedal 8', 4'

  Great to Pedal 8', 4'

  Orchestral to Pedal 8'

  Great to Pedal, reversible

  Swell to Pedal, reversible

  Solo to Great, reversible

ACCESSORIES

  Crescendo Pedal, adjustable, not moving registers

  Balanced Swell Pedal

  Balanced Great and Orchestral Pedal

  Balanced Solo and Celestial Pedal

  Sforzando Pedal

  "The Mechanism of the Swell Pedals so arranged that they may be worked as a MASTER PEDAL, operating all the swell boxes at one time."

COMBINATIONS

  10 adjustable General pistons over upper manual

  6 adjustable foot pistons for Pedal[39]

1926 CHANGES AND ADDITIONS

GREAT ORGAN

  Major Diapason 8', 73 pipes [37; large scale, on new chest]

  Mixture 5 ranks, 305 pipes [15th-17th-19th-22nd-29th, on new chest]

  Keraulophone 8', 73 pipes [52; present enclosed chest]

GREAT ORGAN (cont.)

  Gemshorn 8', 73 pipes [49 taper; 12 new trebles, present enclosed chest]

  [Principal 4' moved to open section]

  [Fifteenth 2' moved to open section]

SWELL ORGAN

  English Diapason 8', 73 pipes [43; on present chest]

  Wald Horn 8', 73 pipes [Capped Tuba scale]

  Gedeckt 8', 61 pipes [small scale, on new chest]

  Plein Jeu IV [replaced Cornet]

ORCHESTRAL ORGAN

  Horn Diapason 8', 73 pipes [46; on present chest]

  Melophone 8', 73 pipes [12 new st. bass and 12 new top octave pipes]

  Double Oboe Horn 16', 12 pipes [4" scale bottom octave, present chest]

SOLO ORGAN

  Stentogamba 8', 73 pipes [8' Violone scale, on present chest]

  Gambette 4', 73 pipes [on present chest]

  French Horn 8', 73 pipes [6" scale, on present chest]

ECHO ORGAN

  Flauto Dolce 8', 73 pipes [replaced Viole Aetheria]

  Flute Celeste 8', 61 pipes [replaced Dolce Celeste]

PEDAL ORGAN

  Major Diapason 16'/Open Diapason 8', 44 pipes [lg. scale; new chest]

  Gedeckt 16'/8', 44 pipes [Sub bass scale, on new chest]

  Lieblich Dolce (II Ranks) [new borrow action for Dolce 8', with Lieblich Gedeckt 16' of Orchestral Organ]

  New set of Class A Chimes [Deagan] to be furnished; old tubes to be returned.[40]

  [N.B.: It would seem that two sets of pipes (the Gemshorn and Melophone) were not new, and were apparently stops saved from the Kimball organ.]

COUPLERS AND ACCESSORIES ON THE 1937 CONSOLE

COUPLERS

  Great to Great 16', 4'

  Swell to Great 16', 8', 4'

  Solo to Great 16', 8', 4'

  Orchestral to Great 16', 8', 4'

COUPLERS (cont.)

Orchestral to Orchestral 16', 4'

Swell to Orchestral 16', 8', 4'

Solo to Orchestral 16', 8', 4'

Solo to Great 8' (reversible)

Solo to Solo 16', 4'

Great to Solo 16', 8', 4'

Swell to Solo 8', 4'

Solo to Pedal 8', 4'

Swell to Pedal 8', 4' (8' reversible)

Great to Pedal 8', 4' (8' reversible)

Orchestral to Pedal 8' (reversible)

Pedal to Pedal 8'

ACCESSORIES

Same as in 1915 Console, except that Great and Orchestral now had separate swell pedals.

ADJUSTABLE COMBINATIONS

8 to Great and Pedal

4 to Celestial/Great; 4 to Celestial/Solo

8 to Swell and Pedal

8 to Orchestral and Pedal

8 to Solo and Pedal

5 to Pedal (toe pistons)

14 General (5 duplicated in toe pistons)

"ON/OFF" for switching Solo and Celestial

General Cancel[41]

1940 CHANGES AND ADDITIONS

GREAT ORGAN

Second Octave 4' [made by adding 9 pipes to old (Kimball?) Twelfth]

Twelfth 2 2/3' [new]

Fourniture V Rks [new]

Mixture IV Rks [old 5-rank Mixture with a rank removed]

SWELL ORGAN

Sesquialtera IV [new]

Trompette 8' [new]

ORCHESTRAL (CHOIR) ORGAN

Fugara 4' [new? or from Kimball?]

Nasard 2 2/3' [new]

Tierce 1 3/5' [new]

[Melophone removed, presumably to make room for additions listed above]

PEDAL ORGAN

Octave 4' [new?]

Super Octave 2' [new?]

Mixture IV Rks [new][42]

[*The Diapason* gives the pitches for the Octave and Super Octave as 8' and 4' and adds a 4' Flute, but the list above, taken from the Austin files, is probably more accurate.]

ALTERATIONS MADE WHEN THE AUSTIN ORGAN WAS MOVED TO PROVO IN 1948

Celestial, String, and enclosed Great divisions were removed entirely.

At least four full-compass stops and two wood basses were removed from various manual divisions, for planned use the in Æolian-Skinner organ.

Internal arrangement was altered from "single-storey" to "two-storey" to fit the chamber in the auditorium.

NOTES

1. Letter to the Austin Organ Co., Sept. 6, 1916.
2. Austin Organ Co. contract, dated Mar. 18, 1915.
3. *Deseret Evening News*, Mar. 18, 1915.
4. Letter to Herbert Brown, Mar. 26, 1915 (Austin files).
5. *Journal History*, May 11, 1915.
6. Orpha Ochse, *The History of the Organ in the United States*, Chapter 12 (Bloomington, IN, 1975).
7. *A List of Organs Installed or Under Construction.* Austin Organ Co. (Hartford, n.d.).
8. N. LaVerl Christensen, *Provo's Two Tabernacles* (Provo, 1983).
9. Letter to Percival Stark, Sept. 10, 1915 (Austin files).
10. *Journal History*, Dec. 10, 1915.
11. Ms. notes in Tabernacle organ file, Austin Organs, Inc.
12. *Journal History*, Dec. 2, 1924.
13. Letter to Herbert Brown, Mar. 30, 1915 (Austin files).
14. Ibid.
15. Letter to Tabernacle Organ Committee, Apr. 7, 1915 (Austin files).
16. *Journal History*, May 17, 1916.
17. *Journal History*, Nov. 14, 1915.
18. *The Great Organ of Salt Lake City*, Austin Organ Co. (n.d.).
19. *Journal History*, Jan. 8, 1916.
20. *Deseret News*, July 13, 1936.
21. *The Great Organ*, op. cit.
22. *Journal History*, May 11, 1916.
23. *Deseret News*, May 12, 1916.

24. Alexander Schreiner, *Alexander Schreiner Reminisces* (Salt Lake City, 1984).

25. *The Great Organ*, op. cit.

26. *Deseret News*, Dec. 10, 1915.

27. Austin Organ Co. contract, op. cit.

28. *The Great Organ*, op. cit.

29. "John J. M'Clellan Dies of Paralytic Stroke," *The Diapason*, Vol. 16, No. 10 (Sept. 1925).

30. "Salt Lake City Organ Will Grow to 131 Stops," *The Diapason*, Vol. 17, No. 3 (Feb. 1926).

31. Tabernacle organ file, Austin Organs, Inc.

32. *Deseret News*, Sept. 10, 1926.

33. John Longhurst, "The Salt Lake Mormon Tabernacle Choir." *The American Organist*, Vol. 22, No. 12 (Dec. 1988).

34. Frank W. Asper, "Salt Lake City Organ, Long a World Wonder, Wins New Attention." *The Diapason*, Vol. 28, No. 5 (Apr. 1937).

35. "Making Additions to Famed Mormon Tabernacle Organ." *The Diapason*, Vol. 32, No. 4 (Mar. 1941).

36. A. Schreiner, Letter in *The Diapason*, Vol. 31, No. 4 (Mar. 1940).

37. Schreiner, *Reminisces*, op. cit.

38. Letter from J. B. Jamison to Austin Organ Co. (Austin files).

39. *The Great Organ*, op. cit., and annotated contract from files of Austin Organs, Inc.

40. Contract signed Dec. 15, 1925, in files of Austin Organs, Inc. (with supplementary notes on Swell mixture).

41. *The Great Organ of Salt Lake City*, Austin Organ Co., 1943.

42. Tabernacle organ file, Austin Organs, Inc.

*The leadership team
for the Æolian-Skinner Tabernacle
organ installation;
seated (l. to r.): Alexander Schreiner,
G. Donald Harrison, Stanley Williams;
standing (l. to r.): Leland Van Wagoner,
Martin Carlson, Herbert Pratt*

The Æolian-Skinner Organ Opus 1075, 1948

I still think that Salt Lake City is the finest organ that I have built so far and will probably remain that way. Of course, the place has marvelous acoustics from the organ point of view.[1]

G. DONALD HARRISON

Alexander Schreiner and Frank Asper served jointly as Tabernacle organists, with Wade N. Stephens as assistant, from the late 1930s through the war years. They were joined by a third colleague, Roy M. Darley, in 1947. It was Schreiner, however, who appears to have set in motion the plans that eventually led to a new organ for the Tabernacle. Shortly after Austin had completed the 1940 alterations, Schreiner was discussing further changes with Stanley W. Williams, the Pacific Coast representative of the Æolian-Skinner Company, who seems to have been the agency through which a new English Horn was added to the Solo division. In 1944 Schreiner entered into direct correspondence with G. Donald Harrison of the Boston firm, and early in 1945 Harrison was brought to Salt Lake City to evaluate the Tabernacle organ.[2]

Like Ridges, Hedgeland, and the brothers Austin, Harrison was British-born, having received his training with the distinguished Henry Willis firm in London. In July 1927 he joined the E. M. Skinner Company in Boston (shortly to be renamed Æolian-Skinner following the acquisition of the Æolian Company).

In 1933 he became the firm's technical director, and in April 1940 he was elected its president.[3] Under his direction in the late 1930s the firm had steadily moved away from the "symphonic" tonal concepts of the firm's founder to the more integrated and eclectic ideal that would soon become known as "American Classic." In the process, Æolian-Skinner had become the builder of choice for many of the more avant-garde organists and had secured many prestigious contracts with educational institutions and large urban churches.

Although Harrison was initially approached to recommend and carry out further tonal improvements, he was not enthused about having to work with the old mechanism and pipework. But on his visit he was greatly impressed by the many roles the Tabernacle organ was required to play and even more impressed with the fabled acoustics of the place: "I find that they are more perfect than I expected. This means that the sound of any organ pipe, particularly when located in the commanding position occupied by the organ, is mellowed and beautified to an extraordinary degree."[4] In March, Harrison sent Bishop Ashton a proposal for an organ that would be completely new mechanically, and very nearly so tonally.

Harrison's proposal was enthusiastically supported by Schreiner and Asper. A lively correspondence between Harrison and Schreiner followed for the next few months in which many of the preliminary tonal and mechanical details were hammered out. A new Antiphonal division in the rear gallery was proposed, and various details of stops, mechanisms, and console appointments were discussed, from tremolos and signal lights to string scales and mixture compositions. In the process, Schreiner displayed an extraordinary grasp of the technical side of organ building, and Harrison showed an excellent understanding and appreciation of the musical side. Both men dealt patiently and exhaustively with even the most minute details of their mammoth project. Their mutual respect is evident in every page of their correspondence.

In May 1945, Harrison visited Salt Lake City again. His primary purpose was to discuss the contract with Bishop Marvin O. Ashton and Schreiner. He also brought along a box of "experimental pipes" to try in the organ "to see what kind of an effect they have in the Tabernacle."[5] Following his visit, the Tabernacle musicians pressed the First Presidency for a decision on the proposed contract, soliciting support and recommendations from several noted American organists.

In November, Harrison again journeyed to Utah, this time to confirm details of the contract, which was signed shortly afterward by President George Albert Smith. The target date for completion was the spring of 1948. On December 8, 1945, a public announcement of the transaction was made, stating that "the great organ is to be almost wholly rebuilt to make it one of the most versatile instruments in its class in the world," although "the exterior of the organ will not be materially affected."[6] Both statements proved correct. Only two alterations were made to the exterior. The number of front pipes in the flat sections of the 1915 side additions was reduced from five to four, and the nonspeaking central wood pipes were replaced with smaller-scaled metal ones to improve egress for sound.

Writing to a friend shortly afterward, Harrison gave credit to Schreiner for his support in securing the contract:

> Due to the strength of character of Alexander Schreiner, the chief organist, there was absolutely no competition, and he stuck to one theme—that was, that unless one man was placed in charge of the building they would rather carry on with the old instrument with all its faults. Having decided upon the man, he should be given his own way as to the specification after the particular requirements of the Tabernacle were explained to him. Under these conditions, you will see that the whole responsibility has really been placed on my shoulders, and I do not think you will be disappointed with the tonal layout. With the location of the organ and the superb acoustics there is a real chance to build the most distinguished instrument in the country, and that is what I intend to try to do.[7]

The language of the contract confirms Harrison's statements, as well as the faith that Schreiner and his associates placed in Harrison's expertise. A clause inserted into the standard form, probably by the purchaser, reads:

> It is specifically agreed that a substantial and material part of the consideration for this agreement is the skill, knowledge, experience and reputation of G. Donald Harrison in the design, construction, finishing, installation, and tuning of pipe organs; that the builder, therefore, enters into this agreement with the distinct and definite understanding that the Purchaser shall receive, without additional cost to it, the personal supervision and services of the said G. Donald Harrison in the performance of this contract and in particular in the designing, finishing, installing and tuning of said organ.[8]

Harrison seemed to appreciate the opportunity and challenge that this contract represented. In acknowledging his receipt of it, he told Schreiner:

> It is now up to me to deliver the goods. With the location of the organ, and the magnificent acoustics of the Tabernacle, I feel there is a real chance to build the most beautiful organ in the world to date—at least that is what I am going to try to do. I say this not in a boastful spirit, but rather in one of humility.[9]

The postwar period saw a great upsurge in organ building in the United States. Some builders had been unable to ride out the wartime years and had failed. Those remaining had more than enough work, and Æolian-Skinner in particular had a heavy backlog that included a significant number of three- and four-manual instruments. Thus while Harrison and Schreiner remained in constant correspondence, design work for the new Tabernacle organ did not begin in earnest until March 1947. Harrison and Schreiner collaborated on the tonal layout, but Schreiner "diplomatically deferred to Harrison in most matters except console appointments and nomenclature."[10]

Harrison took all suggestions from Schreiner and Asper under careful advisement, accepting some and rejecting others, but only after detailed written discussion. From 1945 to 1947, this interaction between builder and organists, along with Harrison's continuing tonal experimentation, resulted in several changes to the stoplist and refinements in internal arrangements and console appointments. At one early stage Harrison suggested incorporating a free reed stop (Euphone), having seen and liked one in a Roosevelt organ being rebuilt for Indiana University. This idea was later discarded, however. Mixture names and compositions cropped up regularly, alterations evolved, and an extensive correspondence developed over the chimes. A baroque Rankett was added to the Positiv, prompting John Toronto to quip that it must be a misspelling of "Rackett or else Ratchet."[11] Toronto, nearing retirement, had been joined by a younger technician, Leland Van Wagoner, who in 1946 was sent to spend some time at the Æolian-Skinner factory to familiarize himself with the mechanical and tonal details of their instruments.

In 1946, Harrison found time in his busy schedule to experiment with certain stops, notably the Bombarde, and to get samples of the reed stops made and tested. He wrote to Schreiner, "I am sure you will like our Swell Hautbois. It has French shallots, and quite an edgy quality."[12] In early April of the same year Schreiner passed through Boston on a concert tour and discussed console details with Harrison. On this trip he also saw some of Æolian-Skinner's latest work in Worcester and New York.

In December 1946, Harrison wrote Schreiner that preliminary layout work had started:

> I propose to lay out the instrument on a somewhat grand scale with extra wide passage boards and inclined ladders with hand rails rather than vertical ones so that when you feel inclined you can take interested parties through the instrument without being afraid they may break their necks or grasp at the top note of a 16' to lever themselves up to a passage board. It is going to be an exhibition piece, and I think it will be worth while seeing as well as hearing.
>
> I am working very hard on the scaling, and I am getting out an entirely new set of scales for the principal flue work of the instrument as I want to take organ building a step forward with this job.[13]

Harrison later expanded on the matter of his principal scaling:

> I am sure that you will be interested to know that practically none of the scale ratios for the chorus work follow the usual plan of halving on the 17th or 18th note. Rather they are laid out to suit the ear, which requires the pipes to get progressively large in the treble, particularly bearing in mind the fact that we want the trebles to sing. Naturally as the scale increases the cutup will decrease in proportion so as to keep the color present. Another thing that I have avoided . . . is that there are no two pipes of similar length in a single department which have exactly the same scale.[14]

In the same communication quoted above, Harrison also discussed such diverse subjects as the dimensions of the manual keys, the arrangement of the chests, the composition of the Swell mixtures, and what kind of 4' flute to employ in the Positiv. "Perhaps the most successful ones I have built have used the 4′ Nachthorn rather than the Koppelflöte," he wrote.

Actual shop work on the organ seems to have begun around June 1947, but the final scales were not sent to the pipe shop until September 15, and a number of changes were made even after that date.[15] Some of these were additions, fortunately prepared for in the console and chests, made possible by the timely repeal of a 10 percent sales tax on organs. Harrison had just completed another significant project in the summer of 1947, the rebuilding (with major tonal changes) of Walcker's 1863 Boston Music Hall organ, located since 1909 in the Memorial Music Hall of Methuen, Massachusetts:

> The rebuilding of the Methuen organ is just coming to an end, and I must say the full effect of the flue work is quite something to hear. It is overwhelmingly brilliant, and yet you can play for a long period without tiring the ear to any extent. I built up the trebles on this organ. In other words, I was doing quite a little practicing getting ready for Salt Lake City.[16]

As 1947 drew to a close, preparations began to be made for the logistics of installation, and some further additions were suggested involving reuse of older pipes. Harrison concurred with Schreiner's request to retain Kimball's Melophone (as a Claribel Flute) and with Asper's request to retain the old Vox Humana, but decided not to incorporate the large-scaled wooden Major Diapason 16′.

Schreiner visited Boston again in February 1948 and briefly saw the Tabernacle instrument in progress at the factory. Harrison regretted he had not time to see the double-rise reservoirs, which had just been completed and were possibly the result of his recent experience with the Methuen organ. The first shipment of organ parts went to Utah in April, and installation began. A clause in the contract required

the builder to keep "sufficient organ in use" at all times during the installation "so that the regular Sunday radio broadcasts can be carried on without interruption." It took a bit of ingenuity to accomplish this, since, with the exception of the casework and the interior set of 32′ Pedal pipes, the Austin organ had to be completely removed before the new one could be installed.

The problem was solved by completing the Antiphonal division first and shipping it in April, ahead of the rest of the organ. Although this division was intended for a chamber at the back of the balcony, opposite the main organ (Austin's basement "Celestial" chamber having been abandoned), it was temporarily placed to the right of the case, above the choir. This work was done by Stanley W. Williams, Æolian-Skinner's west coast representative, and Leland Van Wagoner, the Tabernacle organ technician:

> The antiphonal organ will be operated from the console of the present organ, and will be located in the choir section. When the new sections are all installed within the organ, the antiphonal organ will be moved to the east end of the Tabernacle and operated on a fifth keyboard of the new console which is scheduled to arrive during the summer from Boston.[17]

With only eight speaking stops (played from two manuals and pedal), the Antiphonal division may have served as an adequate support for the choir, but it must have limited the choice of repertoire for the daily recitals. These, like the broadcasts, continued through the summer while the Schoenstein firm of San Francisco removed the Austin organ to Brigham Young University and the Æolian-Skinner crew began setting up the new instrument. The installation was largely done by Henry Sieberg and Martin Carlson, assisted by Carmelo Fabrizio, finisher Herbert Pratt, Leland Van Wagoner, and, occasionally, people from the Schoenstein firm.[18]

40

Despite the limitations of its size, the Antiphonal proved a reassuring omen of things to come for the organists. Schreiner thought the 4′ Principal a little thin and the Vox Humana not sufficiently mild, but he was unrestrained in his superlatives with regard to the rest of its stops. Calling the Diapason "the finest I have ever heard," he found the Gedeckt (a survivor from Ridges's organ) "perfectly charming," the Trumpet "marvelous," and the Mixture "just right." The strings, he said, "float gorgeously." He had never heard "such a fine Violone," and he liked the "better second harmonic," which gave "better definition" to the Bourdon. The Violone and Bourdon were probably Pedal stops temporarily installed along with the Antiphonal. Otto Schoenstein, who was to remove the old organ to Provo, "wondered what the old organ was thinking now, upon hearing such lovely tone come out of the new."[19]

Shipments of organ parts continued through the summer, and in June the pipes for the Swell were being voiced. Harrison wrote Schreiner to ask his opinions of the effect of the Antiphonal in the building:

> How large does the full ensemble sound in the building? How much of the old Austin would it equal in degree of loudness? . . . How large is the Diapason and Octave as compared with the Austin Great stop of the same class? Could you stand more fire in the Trompette without it becoming too thin and loud?
>
> I am asking these questions to help me with the Swell which we are now voicing. I want to avoid making radical changes on the spot if possible for it will save much time.
>
> My reason for asking about the Trompette is that I have several samples but the one I favor is very snappy, much more so than the one you have which is similar to the original we tried out when I was in Salt Lake City.[20]

Schreiner responded that the Antiphonal produced "a very satisfying volume of sound" considering its small size, perhaps "nearly half as loud as the former organ." The 4′ Principal turned out to be the same scale as a similar stop in the Austin, and he was pleased with the Trompette.[21] Harrison thus decided to "put a little more edge" on the Swell Trompette but to hold back a bit on the Bombarde and Clairon: "There is a large margin for regulation on this new Trompette, so that it will be easy to make it slightly more or less fiery when we come to that part of the work."[22]

The main organ was scheduled to be completed by the semiannual Church conference on October 1, but use of the Tabernacle slowed down the installation work. Back in Boston the elaborate new console got behind schedule and was not shipped until September. The installers worked nights, but the kind-hearted Schreiner saw to it that they had a few breaks. In August he wrote Harrison: "I am taking the men into the mountains for scenery, coolness, and picnic after work tonight. Van Wagoner has promised to fry the steaks."[23] By October, although they had managed to take down the Antiphonal, connect the new console and blower, and finish the Swell with the exception of its reed stops,

> the Great was only partly complete. The Positiv and Choir were not operating and had no pipes. The Pedal had only a few pipes. The Bombarde and Solo were yet to be wired and winded. . . . The October 1 conferees heard six ranks of the Great and most of the Swell while work continued on the rest.[24]

This scenario is reminiscent of another October Church conference a little over eighty years earlier. In 1867, conferees had heard about one-third of the pipes (and those not all in tune) of Joseph Ridges's grand new organ, which nonetheless was, like Æolian-Skinner's, "in a condition to accompany the choir."[25] And Schreiner continued to be pleased with it. After having spent some time tuning the Swell Plein Jeu himself, Schreiner pronounced it "the

41

most musical one I have ever heard. It is beautiful."[26] He also had praise for the Swell reeds.

Like Ridges's men, Æolian-Skinner's installers were working overtime, but some mechanical parts and reed pipes did not arrive until November and December. Not until a few weeks before Christmas was G. Donald Harrison able to do any tonal finishing on the site.[27] Presumably it was on this trip that he wrote back to the factory with some of his first impressions of the instrument, having heard it played by Schreiner from the best vantage point at the rear of the room:

> It has proved my theory that the complex sound composed of many elements, all mild but different, build up to a sound of indescribable grandeur. . . .
>
> The strings are good but not so soul stirring as I hoped for; a trick of the acoustics, I feel, because all are modified.
>
> Please tell the voicers of the great success of their efforts. There is not one regret in the job.
>
> I don't believe anyone will say the job is too loud. It excites the nervous system without permanent injury.[28]

Harrison returned for further work after the holidays, and the organ was dedicated on January 16, 1949, even though it is probable that the usual odd jobs of tidying up loose ends continued a little after this date. One rather important loose end did not get taken care of until 1951, when the Antiphonal division, hastily put into storage in the fall of 1948, was finally installed by Leland Van Wagoner in a specially constructed chamber at the rear of the gallery.

Concerts by the Tabernacle organists and other well-known players followed, and at least one of these was of an impromptu nature. The week the organ was opened, the Utah Chapter of the American Guild of Organists was having its Midwinter Conclave. The noted French organist Marcel Dupré, who had given recitals on the old Austin in 1919 and 1921, had just played a program in Provo and made a special detour to Salt Lake City (en route to his next concert in St. Louis) to see the new organ. Dupré attended Frank Asper's noon recital and afterward was invited to play the instrument. After having lunch as a guest of the Guild, he returned to the organ a second time, undoubtedly much to the delight of his hosts, who were invited to listen. Dupré praised the Tabernacle's acoustics and stated, "The instrument is glorious, and it is in perfect balance."[29]

A little more than a month later, on February 26, the Utah Chapter of the Guild sponsored E. Power Biggs in a varied program of works by Handel, Haydn, Bach, Widor, Mozart, Alain, and Reubke. This program showed off the resources of the new organ, which Biggs declared "an artistic as well as a mechanical masterpiece." An old friend of Asper, Schreiner, and Harrison, Biggs had watched the organ take shape on his occasional visits to the Æolian-Skinner factory. He considered the completed instrument the high point of his concert tour. Praising the organ's tonal balance, he said, "Everything needed to play the works of the classic masters as well as the compositions of the modern composers with their delicate shades of tone color is there, perfectly balanced."[30]

This ideal of balance and eclecticism, which the organ communicated so well to its distinguished visitors, was elaborated on in an address given by G. Donald Harrison at the Guild of Organists Conclave. He outlined the four types of music the organ was designed to play—baroque, romantic, modern, and accompaniments for choral and solo music—and the divisions of the organ best suited to each type.[31] *Balance* is indeed a word that recurs often in references to the Tabernacle organ. After playing the instrument for a decade, Alexander Schreiner wrote:

No one stop, though it be of dominating quality, is allowed to blot out whole sections of weaker voices, so that when the last Tuba is added, the sound is still that of a large organ and not that of one stop accompanied by all the rest. Naturally, there are delicate flue and reed stops which cannot be heard in a full ensemble, but the foundation stops, mixtures, and reeds, which are the backbone of the organ, are so well balanced that each contributes to a "democratic" ensemble of sound.[32]

Shortly before the organ was completed, Schreiner wrote to Harrison, "I have long thought it would be a matter of pride to us, to have your name appear on the console name plate. Perhaps also the year, 1948. If that is possible, we should be very pleased."[33] Harrison complied by providing a signature plate on the right of the nameboard, complementing the company plate on the left. Thus originated a practice that later became customary with Æolian-Skinner. But it is perhaps nowhere more appropriate than on the Tabernacle instrument, which Harrison himself in later years felt to have been his finest work.

Like all its predecessors, the Æolian-Skinner organ was required to be in almost constant use for recitals, broadcasts, recording, practice, and choir rehearsals, resulting in heavy wear on its action. And inevitably as the organists gained greater familiarity with it, minor tonal alterations and adjustments seemed desirable. The first of these occurred not long after the organ was installed, when the Schoenstein firm regulated the Swell reeds and mixtures and a troublesome Rankett in the Positiv. Æolian-Skinner softened the Great Kleine Mixtur in 1953 and revised the Swell Cymbale in the summer of 1957, a year after Harrison's death. Schreiner later had misgivings about the latter alteration.

Dr. Schreiner was responsible for one addition. Having admired a Kimball Vox Humana in the old Assembly Hall organ, he arranged in 1958

for it to be installed in the Swell by Melvin Dunn, the Tabernacle organ technician, on a separate chest provided by Æolian-Skinner, and gave it the fanciful Greek name of "Melos Anthropon." The Bombarde Grosse Cornet was loudened by Æolian-Skinner in 1969, and in the 1970s, after that firm had closed, some reeds were revoiced by the Trivo Company. In 1979 a two-rank celeste was removed from the Solo to provide room for three stops, added by Casavant Frères to create a cornet. Some mechanical work was also performed in this period. Worn relays and keyboards were replaced, and the top of the console was lowered in 1954 to provide the organist a better view of the conductor.[34] The Antiphonal division, still winded from the main blower, was provided with its own blower during the 1960s.

Through the years, redesignings of the organ were proposed by various firms, including the Æolian-Skinner Company shortly before it went out of business in the early 1970s. Fortunately none of these proposals was seriously considered, but by the early 1980s it was clear that a thorough renovation was needed, including some judicious alterations, provided that they did not alter the basic character of the organ. Tabernacle organist Robert Cundick expressed that

> 40 years of extensive experience convinced us that the American Classic aesthetic, so successfully brought to fruition in this instrument, is and will continue to be artistically valid. Yet, there were areas where problems were evident.[35]

The Schoenstein firm of San Francisco had had a long association with the Æolian-Skinner Company and the Tabernacle organ and was asked to survey the instrument in November 1984. Jack M. Bethards, president and tonal director of the firm, met with organists Robert Cundick, John Longhurst, and Clay Christiansen and made a division-by-division evaluation of the instrument from both a tonal and mechanical standpoint. The study revealed a heavily used instrument that was "somewhat showing its age." The console, already on its second set of keyboards, was badly worn, combination actions and relays were giving trouble, and there were wind deficiencies in the Bombarde, Solo, and Pedal. Tonally, the organ was considerably out of regulation, either from haste in the original finishing or from the work done at various times to individual stops, and the pipework was dirty.

Bethards had no desire to impose his own ideas on Harrison's masterpiece, so his approach was conservative: "Make changes only where there is serious need; make additions only if they do not compromise the integrity of the original work."[36] He began by making a thorough study of all documentary material relating to the organ. He also studied other Æolian-Skinner organs of the same period and solicited input from organists who knew the "American Classic" style. In keeping with his understanding of the historical aspect, Bethards and his workers also kept careful daily logs of their work. In the few instances where pipework was removed, it was carefully packed and stored. A detailed account of the work done by the Schoenstein firm appeared in the December 1988 issue of *The American Organist* (see also Appendix A).

Because it was felt that as much specialized knowledge as possible should be brought to bear on the project, Bethards adopted a team approach to the work carried out between 1984 and 1988. Supplementing the Schoenstein staff were members of several other firms whose contributions were vital. Bethards took charge of the console layout, the design and scaling of additions, and the supervision of the voicing and finishing. Steuart Goodwin, Schoenstein's Southern California service representative, did most of the flue pipe regulation and rescaling. Other voicing and regulation was done by Terrence Schoenstein, Robert Rhoads, and Fred Lake. At the Schoenstein factory, reeds were renovated and new metal pipes made by John Hupalo and Thomas Anderson, formerly of the Æolian-Skinner pipe shop. Console renovation, engineering, and construction of new windchests and reservoirs were supervised by Robert Rhoads, factory manager, and Glen Brasel, engineer. New reed pipes came from several sources, including A. R. Schopp's Sons, former Æolian-Skinner pipemaker Roland Dumas, and Austin Organs, Inc., the latter supplying the two high-pressure reed stops that were voiced by David A. J. Broome.

New keyboards that replicated the old were ordered from P and S Organ Supply of England. H. Ronald Poll and Associates of Salt Lake City designed and installed the new solid-state switching system that was made by Solid State Logic, Ltd. of England. A key person in carrying out and coordinating much of the work done in the Tabernacle itself was head organ technician, Robert Poll, along with his associate Lamont Anderson and others of the Tabernacle staff.

It is important to note that most of these changes were in the nature of additions or revoicing. The only stops that were actually removed (besides the Solo Viole Celeste, which was taken out in 1979) were the 8' Melos Anthropon, the Swell 4' Clairon, and the bass octave of the 8' Harmonic Trumpet, the remainder of which became the new 4' Clairon. The new Cavaillé-Coll style 8' Flûte Harmonique in the Great is a particularly successful stop, replacing a similar stop of narrower scale that was moved to 4' pitch. Other flue additions include a Cornet V in the Great, a 2' Hohlflöte in the Swell, and a 2' Principal in the Pedal.

The Swell Plein Jeu VI and Choir Carillon III were divided for greater flexibility, an 8' Montre was added to the Great, and the Positiv was given more foundation by the addition of an 8' Principal and a strong French Cromorne 8'. Even the Positiv Rankett was rehabilitated after it was discovered that most of its problems were caused by some of the chest holes being too small.

Harrison's general practice was to omit reeds in the Great, assuming that strong reeds in other divisions, such as the Bombarde, could be coupled. Bethards, however, felt justified in adding chorus reeds at 16', 8', and 4' pitches after having read some of Harrison's early correspondence. Other reed additions included a second Trompette in the Swell, the previously mentioned Cromorne in the Positiv, and a high-pressure Tuba Mirabilis and Trompette Harmonique based on the work of Harrison's mentor, Henry Willis.

Problems in the wind system were solved by adding or adjusting regulators and concussion bellows and by placing the large Pedal flues on a separate wind supply with a new blower. The electrical system, already altered and patched by earlier repairs, was replaced by a new solid-state system. This system included a multilevel combination action that was sorely needed in an organ regularly used by three organists, two associates, and visiting players. The console was refinished and mechanically rebuilt, with new keyboards, new pedal key covers, and added accessories such as duplicate pedal and thumb pistons. Every effort was made to preserve the original appearance of the console, and electronic-age additions such as the indicator panels above the top manual were thus made as unobtrusive as possible.

A few entirely new features included communications equipment for the organists and tuners, and a built-in fan with adjustable ducts to give relief to organists working under hot television lights in the building, which is not air conditioned. At the suggestion of the organists, the entire console was placed on a rotating disk to facilitate changing its position for different functions. This was designed by Ronald John, supervisor of operations for Temple Square, and constructed and installed by Bonneville Machine, Inc. of Salt Lake City.[37]

The renovation was carried out over a period of four years. During this time the organ remained in regular use, the result of careful planning by H. Ronald Poll and the Tabernacle staff and of the use of a temporary console provided by R. A. Colby, Inc. When the work was finished, the Tabernacle organists and the organ builders felt that a celebration was in order, and plans evolved for an American Classic Organ Symposium to be held January 19-22, 1989, free of charge. Thomas Murray and Robert Glasgow, internationally known recitalists, presented concerts on the evenings of January 20 and 21. Daytime events included historical lectures by Thomas Murray, Robert Glasgow, Jack Bethards, and Barbara Owen; noon and afternoon recitals by Clay Christiansen, John Longhurst, and Robert Cundick; demonstrations of the organs in the Assembly Hall; a bus trip to Brigham Young University; and a gala luncheon on the 26th floor of the Church Office Building. Of the recitals, reviewer Roy Kehl wrote: "In every instance the vast range of tonal color of the Tabernacle organ was explored amply. The programs were sensitively designed, each player was at home with the instrument, and there was much in the playing of depth, richness, and joy."[38]

A large number of organists and music lovers attended this unique event, coming from throughout the United States to make or renew their acquaintance with an instrument that is indeed an "American Classic," not only for the particular period of organ history that it represents, but also because of its roots in more than a century of American organ-building tradition. All symposium events were recorded, and a four-cassette synopsis of the proceedings has been made available through the Educational Resources Library at the national headquarters of the American Guild of Organists.

A stoplist of the Æolian-Skinner organ in its present form, with annotations by Jack Bethards, can be found in Appendix B.[39]

NOTES

1. Letter to Ralph Downes, Sept. 29, 1954.
2. Jack M. Bethards, "Review of the 1948 Installation." *The American Organist*, Vol. 22, No. 12 (Dec. 1988).
3. "G. Donald Harrison Heads Organ Concern." *The Diapason*, Vol. 31, No. 6 (May 1940).
4. Letter to Bishop Marvin O. Ashton, Mar. 9, 1945 (Church Archives).
5. Letter to Alexander Schreiner, May 21, 1945 (Church Archives).
6. *Journal History*, Dec. 8, 1945.
7. Letter to Wm. King Covell, Dec. 11, 1945 (Boston Organ Library).
8. Contract in Church Archives.
9. Letter to Alexander Schreiner, Dec. 10, 1945 (Church Archives).
10. Bethards, op. cit.
11. Letter to G. D. Harrison, Feb. 4, 1946 (Church Archives).
12. Letter to Alexander Schreiner, Oct. 28, 1946 (Church Archives).
13. Letter to Alexander Schreiner, Dec. 18, 1946 (Church Archives).
14. Letter to Alexander Schreiner, Mar. 25, 1947 (Church Archives).
15. Scale sheets from records of Æolian-Skinner Co.
16. Letter to Alexander Schreiner, June 18, 1947 (Church Archives).
17. *Journal History*, Apr. 16, 1948.
18. "Salt Lake City Organ Completely Rebuilt." *The Diapason*, Vol. 40, No. 4 (March 1949).
19. Letter to G. D. Harrison, May 7, 1948 (Church Archives).
20. Letter to Alexander Schreiner, June 14, 1948 (Church Archives).
21. Letter to G. D. Harrison, June 17, 1948 (Church Archives).
22. Letter to Alexander Schreiner, June 23, 1948 (Church Archives).
23. Letter to G. D. Harrison, Aug. 3, 1948 (Church Archives).
24. Bethards, op. cit.
25. *Journal History*, Oct. 6, 1867.
26. Letter to G. D. Harrison, Aug. 3, 1948 (Church Archives).
27. Bethards, op. cit.
28. Letter to Joseph Whiteford of Æolian-Skinner Co., Dec. 1948.
29. *The Church News*, Jan. 19, 1949.
30. *Deseret News*, Feb. 27, 1949.
31. *The Church News*, op. cit.
32. Alexander Schreiner, "The Tabernacle Organ in Salt Lake City." *Organ Institute Quarterly*, Vol. 7, No. 1 (1957).
33. Letter to G. D. Harrison, Aug. 29, 1948 (Church Archives).
34. Bethards, op. cit.
35. Robert Cundick, "The 1988 Renovation—An Organist's Perspective." *The American Organist*, Vol. 22, No. 12 (Dec. 1988).
36. Jack M. Bethards, "The 1988 Renovation—A Builder's Perspective." *The American Organist*, Vol. 22, No. 12 (Dec. 1988).
37. Cundick, op. cit.
38. Roy Kehl, "The American Classic Symposium in Salt Lake City." *The Diapason*, Vol. 80, No. 5 (May 1989).
39. Jack M. Bethards, in *The American Organist*, Vol. 22, No. 12 (Dec. 1988), with additions.

Epilogue

Special is an epithet often applied to the Mormon Tabernacle organ. Thomas Murray, in his lecture of January 21, 1989, called it the *"quintessential* American organ." That is not the same as saying that it is a *typical* American organ, for in fact it is so atypical that it is in a class by itself. Jack Bethards implies this when he says that the Tabernacle organ has a "signature sound."

To no small degree this is the direct result of an extraordinary set of circumstances, thoroughly American in that they are the legacy of the pioneer settlers of Utah, and at the same time thoroughly classical. The Tabernacle building is like no other, with its huge volume, lozenge shape, and rounded ceiling. The incredible clarity that it lends to the sound of the organ has been a gift that every builder who has worked in that space has appreciated. Joseph Ridges's impressive organ case has been another gift, imparting dignified visual identity and allowing the pipes that stand behind it to occupy the same vast space as those who listen to them.

Because of these two factors, the builders who have worked in the Tabernacle were not required to force the speech of their pipes, as they would in a chambered installation in an acoustically dead church. This free and easy pipe speech may well have been what suggested to choirmaster Stephens the "almost human quality" of the original organ's sound—much as we refer today to the "vocal" quality of ancient pipes in some of the old reverberant churches of Europe. Probably no builder appreciated the gifts of the Tabernacle

more than G. Donald Harrison, who for virtually the only time in his life was given the full opportunity to express his conviction—tinctured with his recollections of organs in great spaces in England and Europe—of what an American organ ought to sound like in a truly classic acoustical situation.

Less than a decade after he completed the Tabernacle organ, Harrison was gone, and the idiomatic era to which he contributed so much was fast becoming history. But just as the best work of Schnitger, Silbermann, Antegnati, Cliquot, Cavaillé-Coll, Willis, Hook, Skinner, and all the other legendary names in the history of "the king of instruments" continues to retain its youthful freshness and musical validity, so the Salt Lake Tabernacle organ will continue to remind us of the heights that could be attained by American builders at the meridian of the twentieth century.

*The old Tabernacle and Bowery
(Note the rounded extension
at the rear of the Tabernacle, which
undoubtedly housed Joseph Ridges's
Australian organ.)*

The new Tabernacle under construction
(Note the sandstone pillars and
wooden ceiling truss detail.)

*The Walcker organ
in the Boston Music Hall as it appeared in
Harper's Weekly, December 12, 1863.
This publication was well
known and readily available in
Great Salt Lake City, Utah Territory.*

TABERNACLE ORGAN,
CIRCA 1885
(COMPARE WITH THE WALCKER ORGAN
IN THE BOSTON MUSIC HALL.)

TABERNACLE ORGAN,
CIRCA 1920

TABERNACLE ORGAN CARVING DETAIL
ATOP A 32' PEDAL TOWER
(NOTE THE SIMULATED OAK FINISH
APPLIED TO THE PINE.)

AUSTIN CHEST INTERIOR
IN THE TABERNACLE, CIRCA 1945

Roy M. Darley
at the Second Austin Console,
Circa 1947

Alexander Schreiner

G. DONALD HARRISON
AT THE NEW ÆOLIAN-SKINNER CONSOLE
BEFORE THE TOP WAS LOWERED

*MOVING THE RESTORED CONSOLE
INTO POSITION AFTER ITS ARRIVAL FROM
THE SCHOENSTEIN FACTORY IN
SAN FRANCISCO*

Jack Bethards (L.)
Steuart Goodwin (R.)

*TEMPLE SQUARE IN SPRINGTIME
WITH THE EAST END OF THE TABERNACLE
IN THE BACKGROUND*

*VIEW OF THE ORGAN
FAÇADE FROM THE CONSOLE*

VIEW OF THE TABERNACLE
ORGAN FROM THE SOUTH BALCONY

TABERNACLE ORGAN CONSOLE
(NOTE THE DISC IN THE FLOOR, PERMITTING
THE CONSOLE TO ROTATE.)

*Pipes of the Great
and Positiv divisions*

Hooded Bombarde reeds

BOMBARDE MIXTURES

An original Tabernacle
organ pipe made by Joseph Ridges

VIEW OF ANTIPHONAL PIPEWORK
(NOTE RIDGES'S PIPES, ROOF TRUSSES,
AND SWELL SHADES.)

*32′ Flûte Ouverte pipes made
by Niels Johnson*

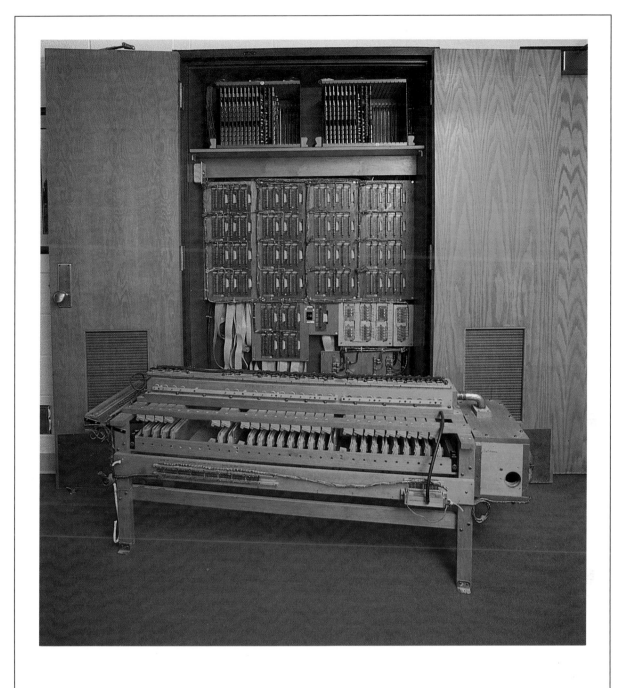

COMBINATION ACTION CLOSET WITH
A SINGLE ÆOLIAN-SKINNER
COMBINATION MACHINE IN THE FOREGROUND.
THE ORIGINAL ÆOLIAN-SKINNER
COMBINATION ACTION CONSISTED OF NINE
MACHINES HOUSED IN A 22' X 10' ROOM.
THE NEW COMBINATION ACTION HAS 64 TIMES
THE CAPACITY OF THE ORIGINAL.

*GREG MORTIMER INSPECTS PIPES
OF THE 32′ BOMBARDE
(NOTE MITRES AND WOODEN PIPE BOOTS.)*

*Upper Great pipework
(Note Cornet V on elevated chest.)*

Blower room

*CLEANING A REED FROM THE
SOLO ENGLISH HORN
(NOTE THE DOLLAR BILL, WHICH PROVIDES
LINT-FREE CLEANING MATERIAL.)*

*METHUEN MEMORIAL MUSIC
HALL ORGAN, FORMERLY
IN BOSTON MUSIC HALL (CF. p. 50)*

Appendix A: The 1984–88 Renovation;
An Organ Builder's Perspective

by Jack M. Bethards
President and Tonal Director
Schoenstein & Co.

Throughout the history of the Salt Lake Mormon Tabernacle organ, the objective has been to have the finest instrument America could produce. American organ builders should note and appreciate that The Church of Jesus Christ of Latter-day Saints has not looked to Europe for organs but has sought instruments that expressed the American eclectic spirit. In reviewing the history of the Tabernacle organs, it seems clear that each new project was reaching toward the goal that G. Donald Harrison was able to realize in 1948—producing a distinguished American organ. When contemplating the renovation in 1984, the Church authorities and organists were clear in their conviction that Harrison's 1948 instrument was their ideal and ultimate instrument. Their desire was simply to complete and perfect it. They felt that after nearly forty years of use, any minor inadequacies should have been discovered. By 1988, the organ's fortieth anniversary, they intended it to be established as a musical landmark on Temple Square, not open to further change. They felt a responsibility as stewards of a national artistic treasure.

We consider the work that was completed in 1988 to be not another step in the organ's evolution but rather a conclusion of Harrison's 1948 project. The word *renovation* was selected carefully to reflect the spirit of renewal rather than rebuilding. This, of course, was an important distinction in designing our work. One clear indication of the seriousness with which we undertook this approach is that no names other than those of G. Donald Harrison

and Æolian-Skinner will be found on the console. We are strongly enough convinced that this instrument has remained true to the Æolian-Skinner tradition that the work can stand on the original nameplates.

1984—RETRACING HARRISON'S STEPS

The Tabernacle Æolian-Skinner is probably the most famous organ in the world. Hundreds of millions of people have heard this organ—perhaps more people than have heard any other organ. More than 2,000 editions of the Tabernacle Choir broadcast, "Music and the Spoken Word," have been carried throughout the United States and in many other parts of the world since 1948. Since its dedication, the organ has been featured on numerous recordings and has been heard daily by visitors to Temple Square in Salt Lake City. For many, this is the sound by which all organs are measured. It is one of the greatest expressions of the American Classic style. It is also one of the largest organs in the world and plays in one of the most favorable settings. For all of these reasons, we approached the Mormon Tabernacle organ with deep respect when, in 1984, we were asked to look into the concerns of the organists, including console problems and tonal matters.

The Schoenstein firm has had a three-generation association with Skinner. It was always the practice of the Schoenstein family to encourage the younger generations to gain experience from the prominent eastern builders. Louis Schoenstein worked for E. M. Skinner, and his son Lawrence was hired by

G. Donald Harrison and stayed with Æolian-Skinner for nearly twenty years. Lawrence's son Terrence was hired by Joseph Whiteford and worked with Æolian-Skinner for several years. The Schoenstein family has also worked at the Mormon Tabernacle going back to the days of the Austin organ. Considering the Schoenstein family's three-generation experience with both Skinner and the Tabernacle, we felt very comfortable contemplating the renovation project.

As I approached Salt Lake City in November 1984 to survey the organ, I wondered what could be wrong with this magnificent instrument—masterwork of G. Donald Harrison. On the other hand, I knew as an organ builder that no artist could ever consider an instrument perfect. The results of placement and acoustics, for example, can never be completely anticipated. Harrison himself certainly had these feelings, and it is well known how often he returned to instruments to make changes—not always minor ones. Organ building is simply too complicated an enterprise to be thoroughly predictable.

I listened to the Tabernacle organists demonstrate the problems they were encountering. Then I went through the organ very carefully to discover the myriad details that made up this grand ensemble that I had listened to for nearly forty years.

The concerns of the Tabernacle organists—all highly skilled players—focused on minor but frustrating limitations. How could an organ that had such a grand overall effect be limited in its variety of individual registrations? For example, the Great organ of thirty-four ranks was usable mainly in combinations employing large numbers of stops. The Super Octave 2′ was almost half the power of the Quinte 2 2/3′. A light principal chorus without mixture was not possible. There was no clear relationship in timbre or volume between the primary and secondary 8′ and 4′ principal stops. Within ranks, there were severe note-to-note regulation problems. Speech was inconsistent. Mixtures tended to be drawn in groups as the individual mixtures evidenced balance problems. In short, the Great, which sounded fine in the hall with massive combinations, did not live up to what a thirty-four-rank Great promised.

Division by division, the organ evidenced the same kinds of limitations. The speech of individual pipes was so irregular that when combined in ensembles, crispness and definition were lost. This was particularly noticeable in the Pedal organ. Some solo stops, including the Swell Hautbois and the Great Flûte Harmonique, were not useful due to regulation or balance problems.

At the end of my lengthy study of the instrument, I became convinced that the organists had legitimate concerns about the tonal properties of the organ. I was equally sure, however, that 95 percent of the problems could be corrected through simple but meticulous tonal regulation. There was clear evidence (later confirmed by research and further inspection) that the organ did not receive quite the kind of thoroughness in tonal finishing that was considered normal for Æolian-Skinner, and that some adjustments had been made in the instrument's finishing over the years. The result of all this was an instrument somewhat showing its age.

Other problems, including the wind system, exacerbated this tonal picture. The blower was not quite adequate to sustain the tutti. This was so marginal that it was hard to pinpoint why the organ seemed to lack excitement when played "full out." Many divisions and subdivisions had terribly unsteady wind, which resulted in poor attack. The Bombarde reeds and Solo Tuba, for example, shook like jelly, robbing them of impact.

There is probably not a large instrument in the world that does not suffer from some internal placement problems. The Tabernacle organ is no exception. Very careful attention to balances in tonal finishing is required to alleviate these problems. In many cases this was not taken into account originally, and in other cases subsequent refinishing had upset some critical relationships.

The world-famed acoustics of the Mormon Tabernacle have some interesting and unexpected characteristics relative to organ tone. First, the building is so vast (seating more than 6,000) that sound energy is somewhat reduced in immediate impact although it carries at that reduced level beautifully throughout the building. Second, the room tends to blend the sound so that almost anything sounds attractive at a distance but may not work as well close up or over the air. Third, sounds from approximately 4' F down diminish in intensity. The shell of the building is plaster on wood frame. Bass frequencies are partially absorbed.

One major point that soon became evident was that the instrument tended to have a center of gravity around 4' pitch rather than 8'. Throughout the work in regulation and additions, great effort was made to add resources that would allow the lowering of this musical center of gravity as needed.

Although great pains were taken in the original design to achieve divisional independence and balance, some of the plans did not work out in actual practice. This was particularly noticeable in the Great and Positiv and somewhat evident in the Pedal. The Swell reed chorus was not in balance with itself or with the ensemble.

Some additional solo stops, including a commanding reed, seemed appropriate for an organ of this scope. Some couplers and registration aids that are especially helpful for the varied and demanding repertoire of the music program were missing.

Finally, the console was beginning to show significant wear. No console in the world gets more heavy and regular use than that of the Mormon Tabernacle organ—seven days a week for recitals, practice, rehearsals, broadcasts, recordings, and tuning. It was already on its second set of Æolian-Skinner manual keys. The relay was causing unnerving lapses in performance. The combination action was beginning to give trouble, but more important was the need for multiple memories, given the increasing demands on the Tabernacle schedule for rehearsal time and the increased participation of associate and guest organists.

PLANNING

The musicians were clearly not able to live with the status quo. They had been working with the instrument for many years and had formed their opinions thoughtfully. They had reached a consensus that work was needed. On the other hand, they loved the organ and respected the men—Alexander Schreiner and G. Donald Harrison—who had planned and built it.

Our first job was to set an overall philosophy to guide us in forming recommendations. This philosophy became clear: make changes only where there is a serious need; make additions only if they do not compromise the integrity of the original work.

RESEARCH

Although the organ had been in use for nearly four decades and one might assume that all of its secrets had been learned simply by testing its musical utility, we firmly believed that no changes could be considered until we knew everything we could about the intent of the original builder. We started by collecting every piece of written information about the instrument we could locate. Through former Æolian-Skinner employees and through the courtesy of the Rodgers Organ Co., which now owns many of the Skinner records, we obtained volumes of correspondence, shop notes, and work orders.

Next we went through the historical archives of The Church of Jesus Christ of Latter-day Saints and obtained Alexander Schreiner's lengthy and detailed files, which covered the history of the organ from his first conversations with Harrison. Allen Kinzey of the Nicholas-Bradford Organ Company and formerly of Æolian-Skinner was very helpful in providing information from his extensive files. He is a dedicated Æolian-Skinner specialist. We interviewed or corresponded with everyone we could find who was connected with the original project, including former Tabernacle organists Alexander Schreiner and Roy Darley.

Finally, we visited Æolian-Skinner organs that either had an influence on the Tabernacle organ or were contemporary with it. This, coupled with the working files of the maintenance staff and our own extensive E. M. Skinner and Æolian-Skinner records, gave us an important resource in all the critical decisions made about the instrument. As the project continued, people who shared our interest in the organ and in Æolian-Skinner contributed material to our rapidly growing files. We have accumulated a great deal of historical and technical information that is fascinating.

Early in the process, two internationally known artists who are experts with respect to E. M. Skinner and Æolian-Skinner organs, Robert Glasgow of the University of Michigan and Thomas Murray of Yale University, both spent

time with the instrument and offered their comments. These ranged from tonal matters to details of console appointment.

METHODOLOGY

At the outset of this work, we established several guidelines that were followed meticulously:

1. Documentation. A day-by-day, hour-by-hour log was kept of everything done to the organ. This includes notations of all regulation in every stop (careful descriptions of the status before work started, inspection notes, experimental procedures, work done, and final results).

2. Archival retention. In those few cases where changes were made, every pipe that was removed from the instrument was labeled, packed, and placed in permanent storage near the Tabernacle. Changes were made in such a·way that they could be reversed if future generations wish to return any portion of the instrument to its original state. For example, in repitching the Pedal mixtures, the 5 1/3′ rank was removed to storage. We removed with it the original toe board and rack rather than adapting them to the new pipes. Although an entirely new toe board and rack had to be made matching the original in finish, we felt this investment was worthwhile to ensure that the change could be reversed with absolute accuracy. This system was followed throughout the project in all changes, whether mechanical or tonal.

3. Differentiation of additions. There are two approaches to the mechanical side of making additions to an existing instrument. One approach is to make the additions appear as though they were part of the original, and the other is to make them clearly different. The former approach gives the instrument a

uniform appearance and the impression that the additions could have been part of the original. The latter approach shows future generations clearly what was original and what was added. Although the instinct of the craftsman is to challenge his skill in making the final product a perfectly finished whole, the historian's approach won out. We decided to make all additions in style of construction and finish to our normal standards. This was also true of the Casavant additions made in 1979. So future historians studying this organ will benefit from a clear picture.

4. Experimentation. From the outset, it was agreed that this work would be under no time pressure except for a general goal of completing it on or about the organ's fortieth anniversary in 1988. The Church encouraged a process of deliberate, step-by-step experimentation for making each decision about tonal changes. This was true of what would seem to be even minor points. Our normal procedure was to start with a written rationale for any tonal change or addition. We then made and tried sample pipes. For example, in connection with the Swell reed chorus, eleven different trials were made. Experimental solutions were evaluated by the organists along with us, sometimes over a long period of time, to dilute first impressions. After completing work, we all agreed to keep an open mind and study the results for a reasonable amount of time before considering it a permanent part of the organ. We had the opportunity of hearing the organ in recital each day. Organists would often arrange to play repertoire that would demonstrate our work in various musical contexts. This immediate feedback was of great value.

There is an interesting parallel in the timing of the 1948 and 1988 projects. Harrison began his discussions with Schreiner in 1944. Our work was started in 1984. Harrison's work was finally completed on January 16, 1949, and the celebration of the completed renovation began on January 19, 1989, with the start of the American Classic Organ Symposium. The thorough and deliberate approach to the renovation project can be noted in the fact that tonal regulation, addition of seventeen ranks of pipes, console and electrical system renovation, and other work was spread over the same amount of time it took originally to design and build the entire instrument. We hope that the result reveals this meticulous approach.

5. Team approach. Members of the Schoenstein & Co. staff were all honored to be involved in this work. Tonal design, scaling of additions, and console layout were done by the writer, who also supervised all tonal work. Steuart Goodwin, Southern California representative of Schoenstein & Co. and a respected builder and restorer, did most of the flue pipe regulation and planned all rescaling of existing pipework. He worked closely with me and the organists on every artistic decision. His sure musical judgment and consummate skill were critical to the success of this undertaking. Other flue regulation was by Terrence Schoenstein and Robert Rhoads. Reed regulation was by Robert Rhoads. Reed renovation was by John Hupalo with voicing by Robert Rhoads. Metal pipes were made by Thomas Anderson, who formerly supervised the Æolian-Skinner pipe shop for eighteen years, and by John Hupalo. Voicing of flue pipes was by Fred Lake. Engineering for all additions was by Glen Brasel. Components, including chests and reservoirs, were made

under the supervision of Robert Rhoads, Schoenstein factory manager, who also directed the console renovation and all installation in Salt Lake City. Other key Schoenstein staff members were Philip Browning, David Fortin, Renato Guerrero, Gayle Holmlund, Eldon Ives, Elmer Ives, George Morten, Dolores Rhoads, Scott Rosencrans, Bert Schoenstein, Don Siler, Leonard Warren, Ronald Warren, and Daniel Yonts. Lawrence Schoenstein served as general consultant.

We considered ourselves the overseers of the project but used other firms and individuals to make up the best expert team possible for this critical assignment. For example, David A. J. Broome, vice president and tonal director of Austin Organs, is one of the world's leading experts in high-pressure reed work. We commissioned Austin Organs to build the pipes and chests for the two high-pressure reeds. High-pressure reservoirs were made by the Crome Organ Company of Los Angeles. A. R. Schopp's Sons of Alliance, Ohio, who had supplied many reeds to the Æolian-Skinner Company, made the chorus reed stops. Roland Dumas, formerly of Æolian-Skinner and C. B. Fisk, made the Cromorne 8′ for the Positiv. New manual keyboards were made by P & S Organ Supply of Brandon, Suffolk, England. The Salt Lake City firm of H. Ronald Poll and Associates accomplished the technical design and installation of solid-state equipment furnished by Solid State Logic and the temporary console built by R. A. Colby.

An indispensable element in this team approach was the contribution of the in-house Tabernacle organ maintenance staff, headed by Robert Poll. With the assistance at varying times of Melvin Dunn, Greg

Mortimer, and Lamont Anderson, Robert helped with the renovation program in addition to the regular duties of tuning and maintaining all of the instruments on Temple Square. This provided an interchange of ideas that produced a practical, serviceable end result. This project could not have been accomplished or the results preserved without the dedication of these fine technicians.

A final indication of teamwork was the smooth working relationship with the three Tabernacle organists and the Church administration. Organ builders shudder at the thought of coordinating the ideas of several artists and managers, but in this case the process couldn't have been smoother. The musicians always considered decisions as a group and reached a clearly voiced consensus. We wish also to acknowledge the invaluable assistance of Ronald John, who served as the vital liaison between us and the Church authorities to ensure their complete understanding and support during the entire project.

TONAL WORK

As soon as the renovation project was announced, people who admired the instrument became worried that it would be revoiced or, even worse, rescaled. Another historic organ would be lost, they feared. It was inspiring to know how much the instrument meant to so many. It was also humorous to hear supposedly authoritative accounts of the work from people who had no direct contact with it. Comments ranged from "they are turning it into a screaming neo-baroque monstrosity" to "they are over-refining it—reducing it to a romantic gray blob." Such is the organ world. Thank goodness, people are concerned. However, it is important to set the record straight now that the work is complete and this written description can be supported with a finished result that stands on its own merits.

All parties embraced the following tonal ideals: reverse changes subsequent to Harrison's 1948 design that had proven inappropriate, correct any faults of aging, carry out the kind of meticulous tonal regulation that Æolian-Skinner would have done with the proper time and budget, and make changes or additions only if they completed preparations already made or solved some long-standing, clearly recognizable musical problem.

Any historian could subscribe to most of that statement. But the difficult questions are who decides what is a major musical problem, and how is that problem corrected. We felt that any builder would relish the opportunity to come back to an instrument after it has had a nearly forty-year trial period, reevaluate it, and solve any problems that had emerged. None of us connected with the project could or would try to second-guess G. Donald Harrison. However, we did try to fortify our decisions with every bit of information we could gain about his approach. We spent well over a year before we formalized any plans for tonal additions. During that time, we worked with the instrument doing tonal regulation, listening to innumerable tests, studying the organ in recital and weekly broadcasts, and meeting with the organists.

This is, I suppose, an ideal way to complete an instrument. What a luxury it would be to install an organ and "rough it out" and then live with it for a year, hearing excellent musicians play it in recital daily, trying various solutions and not being under pressure to finish until everything fit into place. We hope that the final result of all the tonal work will *not* be noticed. This may seem a surprising goal, but we believe that someone who has not

heard the organ for a few years and has not memorized the stoplist could return now and assume that the instrument was original.

Before describing the work, some terms that are often misunderstood should be defined:

1. Scaling. Scaling involves all aspects of the physical design of pipes. Although the major part of this function is determining the diameters of each pipe throughout the compass of the rank, there is much more involved. Determining mouth width, languid bevel, materials and their thickness, shape, and so forth, are all part of the process. For reeds, details of shallot construction and size are also critical. Rescaling means changing one or more of these basic design factors in an existing set of pipes by cutting a pipe apart and remaking it, or, perhaps, by moving it to a different position in the compass and making a new pipe to fill its place. For example, the relative diameter of a rank of pipes can be reduced by removing low C, moving C-sharp through top C down, lengthening them, and then adding a new C at the top of the compass.

2. Voicing. A pipe fresh from the pipe shop usually does not speak at all. The process of voicing is bringing the pipe to speech and then giving it the character and volume that the designer of the organ had in mind when he scaled it. Voicing involves major adjustments to the pipe's structure and to dimensions such as the height of the mouth, the size of the toe and flue openings, and the treatment and position of the languid. Reed voicing is especially complex, involving determination of the relative length of the tongue and resonator and of the size, thickness, weight, shape, and curve of the tongue. When a pipe is revoiced, its character is changed significantly. Revoicing flues may

even involve cutting a pipe apart to lower its mouth or change its languid. For reeds, revoicing often involves new tongues of different thickness, weight, and curve.

3. Finishing. The term *finishing* simply means to put the polishing touches on the voicer's work. Whether the process of voicing is accomplished in a voicing room or in the church, this process of further refinement is still necessary. Finishing involves the same techniques as voicing with three differences. (1) It usually employs two people—a voicer and a finisher (often the tonal director who designed the organ, scaled the pipes, and directed the voicing). (2) Individual ranks are judged in ensemble. At the stage of finishing, when most pipes are in place, the organ can be heard in its entirety and in its environment for the first time. (3) The work is more detailed.

Perhaps 80 percent of voicing work is done in the voicing room, but the last 20 percent of finishing in the church is often the making or breaking of an organ. The finisher judges the organ at the console and in the room and directs the voicer from the overall musical point of view. This role is much like the role of a conductor. Establishing balances within ranks, within subdivisions and divisions, and among all the elements of the full ensemble is the tonal finisher's job. Refinishing is often required when the acoustical environment is changed.

4. Regulating. Regulation is the minor adjustment to an already voiced and finished pipe to alter volume and speech (and to some extent timbre). This involves cleaning, making minor adjustments to toe and flue openings, and occasionally making adjustments in languid and lip position. For reeds, regulation usually requires adjustment of the

relative length of the resonator and tongue, and it can include recurving or replacing tongues that have become damaged or fatigued.

The emphasis here is on the word *minor*. Tonal regulation cannot change the underlying work of the voicer or finisher. Why, then, is regulation needed? Time takes a toll on organ pipes—particularly on those that are voiced on the low-cut, slow-side style. Languids change position (large ones can sag, small ones can pop up), upper and lower lips can shift position or be damaged, dust and dirt can fill flues, and so on. Reed tongues and shallots can be damaged or fatigued. Shallots and tuning wires can loosen. Tuning scrolls can fatigue. Dust and dirt can upset tongues. Chest or action characteristics can change slightly. A competent tuner is always listening to the speech, timbre, and balance of pipes as well as to their pitch. When one pipe falls out of line with its neighbors, it should be regulated. If this is not done (or if it is done badly), an organ will gradually change in character—sometimes drastically. If this goes too far, it is sometimes difficult to find enough uniform pipes to establish a baseline.

In the work on the Tabernacle organ, regulation (in its strict definition) formed over 95 percent of all the tonal work on the Æolian-Skinner pipework. What little rescaling, revoicing, or refinishing was done is detailed here and in the notes to the stoplist (see Appendix B).

TONAL OBJECTIVES

The architect of an organ must have a thorough understanding of his client's musical requirements. No less is required of a builder who is attempting to restore or enlarge an existing organ. Quickly shifting fads must be separated clearly from long-term goals or else an instrument can become nothing more than a pastiche, reflecting a maze of unrelated tonal ideas. We set out six general tonal objectives. The following chart shows how the tonal work satisfied each one:

1. Restore the original speech, timbre, and balance of each stop.
   Tonal regulation throughout

2. Improve divisional independence and completeness.
   Great Montre
   Great Flûte Octaviante
   Great Reeds 16', 8', 4'
   Swell Hohlflöte
   Positiv Principal 8'
   Positiv Cromorne
   Choir Sesquialtera
   Choir Fife
   Pedal Principal 2'
   Pedal Mixtures

3. Add 8' tone.
   Tonal Regulation
   Great Montre
   Great Flûte Harmonique
   Positiv Principal
   Great, Positiv, Swell, Bombarde, and Antiphonal reeds

4. Provide solo colors to broaden tonal palette.
   Great Flûte Harmonique
   Great Cornet V
   Great Trumpets
   Positiv Cromorne

5. Provide solo reed tone also capable of adding to the climactic character of the full organ.
   Bombarde Trompette Harmonique
   Antiphonal Tuba Mirabilis

6. Move, rescale, refinish, or revoice stops only where absolutely necessary and to solve problems such as tuning stability or egress.

Great Fourniture
Swell Plein Jeu
Swell Cymbale
Swell Chorus Reeds (16', 8', 4')
Swell Voix Humaine
Choir Rauschpfeife
Positiv Rankett
Bombarde Grande Fourniture
Bombarde Trompette and Clairon
Solo upper work
Pedal Kornett

The tonal elements in the preceding list will be discussed under each type of work from regulation through additions.

TONAL REGULATION, REFINISHING, REVOICING, AND RESCALING

Our first step was to determine the extent to which problems could be solved by simple regulation. To find out whether this conservative approach would be satisfactory, we performed some preliminary tests.

Steuart Goodwin and I asked the organists to point out the stop that seemed to them the most useless. They unanimously nominated the 8' Diapason of the Bombarde (in effect, the First Diapason of the Great in Harrison's concept). We carefully regulated the stop for proper speech and consistency of timbre. This process involved absolutely no revoicing whatsoever. What was a dull and lifeless stop with gulpy speech and irregular loudness through the compass became the rich and vibrant stop that Harrison must have had in mind. The experiment was so successful that Robert Cundick changed his registrations for the following Sunday's choir broadcast, using the once-shunned stop in several combinations and as a solo voice. We carried this experimental process through several more stops until it became absolutely clear that the rich material of Harrison's original plan was all there to be rediscovered. Certainly there would be no need for any massive changes.

We wanted hands-on experience tuning this huge organ in order to know it well. There is no other way. Working in double shifts with two assistants, Robert and Dolores Rhoads of our firm tuned the entire organ in five days. The detailed information this provided about problems of tuning and regulation proved invaluable in our future regulation work.

On subsequent visits we went through the entire organ, regulating division by division. Stops that were thought to be hopeless came alive. Detailed regulation of the mixture work was fascinating and revealing. In the process, each rank was heard individually as others were muted off. We immediately discovered what we had supposed: much of the mixture work had not been regulated in detail and some had been regulated initially but was upset through changes over the years. Most of the mixture pipes were out of speech. Breaks were rough, and quint/unison balance changed radically through the compass. Many pipes were entirely silent. (Some of these had been muted purposely due to poor speech or drawing. In a few cases, chest actions were not functioning for individual notes because the borings were plugged with original shellac sizing.)

It was a grueling but rewarding process to regulate these mixtures one by one. It is especially true in mixture work that pipes must be precisely on speech and in balance to work as an ensemble. Often a mixture that seems lifeless has simply fallen out of regulation. This was proved over and over again at the Tabernacle as pipes were put into good speech, and the effect was more power and brightness without any revoicing or change in general volume level. This must have been what the

mixtures were like when the organ was new, or what they were intended to be.

The Great Kleine Mixtur had been softened to the point of flutiness. It was unsteady and difficult to tune, and many pipes had been muted. Refinishing to a more normal level, where the pipes spoke comfortably, restored the elegance of this stop. The Swell Cymbale worked far better, also, when it was brought back to its former dynamic level and scale. A slight scale change was made in the Choir Rauschpfeife, but this was purely for tuning stability.

The Bombarde mixture benefited from muting of doubles and $5 \, 1/3'$ pitches, as well as normal regulation. The Great Fourniture 2' was recomposed slightly for similar reasons. Harrison himself changed his ideas about these matters in instruments that postdate the Tabernacle organ.

The Pedal Grand Harmonics $10 \, 2/3'$ was another revelation. It appeared never to have been finished, and, being out of balance, it did not produce the proper effect of a soft 32' when combined with a 16' voice. After regulation, the stop, which is composed of stopped, open, and tapered pipes, became a most useful addition to the wide variety of Pedal 32' options and a grand augmentation of them. All of this work is detailed in the notes to the stoplist (see Appendix B).

The Pedal mixtures were rarely used except in the fullest of combinations. The lower Pedal mixture with its prominent $5 \, 1/3'$ pitch was too strong to serve in medium combinations, and the upper Pedal mixture could not be used without support of the lower. It was all or nothing, and all was too much. We repitched the mixture series by one level, starting at 4'. No changes were made other than simple regulation, the removal to storage of the

5 1/3' rank, and the addition of a 1/3' rank. This greatly increased the range of usefulness of the Pedal mixtures. Although the upper mixture is still best used with the foundation of the lower, the lower mixture can now be used alone. This revision and the addition of the Pedal Principal 2' have made the Pedal organ truly independent.

Some pipework, especially reeds, required mechanical repairs. Most of the manual chorus reeds were sent to San Francisco for renovation—*not* revoicing (see the stoplist notes in Appendix B for details). Pipes were cleaned, scrolls repaired, new tuning wires fitted, shallots tightened, and so forth. Tongues were replaced or recurved only where damaged. Careful measurements and marks were made to ensure that the pipes were left as close as possible to the original intention of Oscar Pearson, Æolian-Skinner's brilliant head reed voicer. Sample pipes were held out to use as models on the voicing machine; then they were renovated at the end of the process. The shallots of the Bombarde Trompette 8' and Clairon 4' had been partially filled with solder in 1977 and were returned to normal. Tongues, which were only very slightly changed in thickness in 1977, were retained. The result was an excellent match between the original Trompette 16' and the two sets that had been brightened. The restored darker tone lends much nobility to the Bombarde chorus, and adequate power is now provided by the new Trompette Harmonique.

Details of pipe racking can alter regulation and stability. The Tabernacle technicians went through the entire instrument, enlarging rack borings where they were too tight to accommodate seasonal changes in humidity; tightening, retaping, and felting tie racks; and so forth. The technicians also felted tuning scrolls as needed on both reeds and large flues. The so-called European-type racking system, similar to the system used for the Schoenstein additions of chorus reeds, was also applied to the Swell chorus reeds. This system provides maximum stability and protection for reed pipes.

OTHER TONAL CHANGES

In the annotated stoplist (Appendix B), the reader will find a description of every tonal change made. The only stops in the 1948 instrument that do not remain are:

> Swell: Clairon 4' (and bass of Harmonic Trumpet 8')
>
> Solo: Viole Celeste (II Ranks)
>
> Pedal: Fagot 16' (Swell borrow)

The Swell Clairon and Harmonic Trumpet were never successful. The reed chorus seemed to lack power, especially in the upper registers. Both reeds were worked on, but to little avail. As a partial compensation the Swell Cymbale was softened and changed in composition at Schreiner's request in 1957 to balance better with the reeds. Before touching any pipes, we experimented with the swell shades to be certain that the problem was not merely egress. We tried different amounts and angles of opening and found that, in the room, the shades were most effective as originally planned. We then studied each of these problem reeds.

The Harmonic Trumpet 8' was intended both as a solo stop and to provide an alternate chorus timbre when substituted for the Trompette 8'. It was specified to have English shallots. We found it fitted with standard Æolian-Skinner French shallots, and from all indications this was the case from the time the organ was finished. There was much speculation about this change. It is quite possible that a stop with English shallots was tried and found to be ineffective, considering wind pressure and placement. To test this assumption, we had sample pipes made; then we tried them. We even tried a hooded sample, since Harrison had once thought of hooding many reeds in the enclosed divisions. The results were quite disappointing. This system of providing two contrasting reed choruses with common 16′ (and sometimes 4′) registers works brilliantly on many Skinner organs, but it did not work well under these circumstances. Whether Harrison discovered this as we did, through trial and error, or made a last-minute change in the specifications after tonal finishing of other divisions, we don't know. The Harmonic Trumpet with French shallots, although having more power and brilliance than the English Trumpet would have, did not add much to the ensemble because it was only slightly more fundamental and powerful than the Trompette. Two attempts were made over the life of the organ to further differentiate this stop from the Trompette. Both had proved ineffective. We decided to replace it with a new Trompette of larger scale, which could add weight and power to the Swell reed chorus.

The Clairon 4′ had also been a problem stop. The upper end of the Contre Trompette 16′ had been traded with it many years ago, perhaps at the time of original finishing. The 4′ line lacked power. When we switched the pipes back, the situation was worse. We tried the treble of the Harmonic Trumpet 8′ in the Clairon chest, and it was a more successful solution. Therefore we put into storage the Clairon 4′ and the bass of the Harmonic Trumpet 8′. The treble of the Contre Trompette 16′, which had been revoiced several years before (as the Clairon), was quite successful and we decided not to reverse this work. The new Trompette 8′ serves well as a larger solo stop and to add fundamental power to the original Harrison chorus. Since it is affected by

the sub- and supercouplers, it can serve as an alternate chorus effect. The Swell Cymbale has been reregulated back to its original volume.

In 1979 when the Casavant additions were made to the Solo division, the two-rank Viole Celeste was sacrificed to provide chest and space for the Casavant Nazard stop. Serious thought was given to returning these to the instrument; however, considering the great utility of the upper work in the Solo, particularly after revoicing, and the fact that the original stops were close in scale and effect to other strings in the organ, we decided to leave the 1979 additions in place. The obvious musical utility of the 1979 additions is corroborated by this interesting historical note. Alexander Schreiner asked G. Donald Harrison in a letter dated June 22, 1946, to consider including a 2′ flute in the Solo—"something that will go with the present 8′ and 4′ flutes for Solo purposes."

It should be noted that one stop was added to the organ after 1948 and then removed in 1987. This is a stop with an unusual history and name coined by Alexander Schreiner—the Melos Anthropon. Dr. Schreiner admired the Vox Humana from the old Kimball organ in the Assembly Hall. He requested the Tabernacle organ technicians to add it to the Æolian-Skinner organ. A chest and box with adjustable expression opening were obtained from Æolian-Skinner, and the "Melos Anthropon" was placed in the Swell on the main Swell wind system. Unfortunately the stop was never successful because it lacked a proper tremulant. Since the stop was not original to the 1948 instrument and had not proved useful over the years, the pipes were removed in 1988. However, the wind chest proved to be extremely valuable to the project. The Æolian-Skinner Voix Humaine was originally installed on the main wind chest fed by a special regulator with its own tremulant. Since this system was on slightly higher pressure than the main system, it would sometimes upset the functioning of the pitman chest. In 1988 the special wind system was rechanneled to the former Melos Anthropon chest, and the Æolian-Skinner Voix Humaine was installed on it. The original Voix Humaine chest, was then available for the much needed addition of a 2' flute in the Swell. This migration might have been destined to happen. On June 22, 1946, Schreiner wrote to Harrison, "I am wondering if you might consider putting the Vox on a separate tremolo and perhaps in a separate box as we now have it." Schreiner's later addition of the Melos Anthropon seems to have been an attempt to gain the perfect Vox effect. The original Æolian-Skinner Voix Humaine, which was quite lovely, has been improved in effect by this change and is now one of the most perfect stops of its type to be found. We think Dr. Schreiner would be pleased.

In many cases when we found a solution for one tonal problem, it opened the way for solving another problem. One good example is the Pedal Kornett 2'. Through the years this stop was unstable in tuning and constantly slipped out of regulation. It was placed with the upper Pedal flues rather than with the reed chorus. Thinking of this stop in the classical sense as only a solo voice, one can see the rationale; however, in the Tabernacle it was more commonly desired as a chorus stop. Because of its regulation problems, it was seldom used in either context. There was a blank section exactly the right size for a 2' reed in the Pedal reed chorus chest. We wondered if the builders did not plan for this stop to be in the chorus originally and then changed their minds. Perhaps word of such a change never got to the voicers, because it was obvious when we experimented with the wind pressure that

the pipes were happier and worked much more perfectly on the Pedal chorus pressure of 6 3/16" rather than the flue pressure of 4 5/16". The stop was moved, repaired, and regulated. It now works beautifully in the chorus and every bit as well as a solo stop because placement of the reed chest is no less advantageous than the flue chest. The opportunity opened by the move of the Kornett was the addition of a 2' principal in the Pedal on the old Kornett chest. This seemingly insignificant stop has proved to be of immense value. Formerly there was nothing between the 2' Pedal flute and the huge battery of mixture tone. The Principal 2' stop has bridged the gap.

Some tonal augmentation was possible through the very simple means of separating ranks within compound stops. In several cases throughout the Tabernacle organ, mixtures and other compound stops are located on two or more wind chests where one would not be large enough to accommodate all the pipes. For tuning convenience, in 1988 most of these were provided with switches located in the organ. In two cases, the versatility of the instrument was enhanced by providing these controls on the console. The Swell Plein Jeu of six ranks is a powerful stop containing such a full breadth of the harmonic series in most of its range that Alexander Schreiner was often quoted as saying it could be played alone, creating a convincing Swell principal chorus. The gravity of the lower pitches, however, made it somewhat less useful than a normal Swell mixture. By simply making the upper four ranks available independently as a 1 1/3' Plein Jeu, additional registrational possibilities were introduced.

The Choir Carillon, composed of the pitch series 2 2/3', 1 3/5', and 1', was repositioned on its toe boards to provide, in addition to the original composition, a Sesquialtera of two ranks and a Fife of one rank. The 1' stop was particularly useful in adding a subtle measure of brilliance in certain combinations.

The original Flûte Harmonique 8' on the Great was disappointing. It did not have the bloom with ascending power in the treble that is so critically important for the interpretation of French Romantic literature. Harrison specified a stop of "Cavaillé-Coll scale." The stop does indeed follow fairly closely a typical Cavaillé-Coll scale progression; however, it is the one used most commonly in either small choir organs or as the Flûte Octaviante 4' of a larger instrument. Surely a vast building such as the Tabernacle requires something larger! We decided to provide new Flûte Harmonique pipes from tenor C up based on Cavaillé-Coll's largest progression. We located it on a new chest directly behind the center front pipes of the main case. It now fulfills what we think Harrison might have envisioned when he specified a Cavaillé-Coll-style Flûte Harmonique. The original Æolian-Skinner stop was moved to 4' pitch and extended by one octave and renamed Flûte Octaviante. Thus it serves, without alteration, in the proper role its scale dictates. Furthermore it provides open flute tone at 4' pitch on the Great—something that should not be absent from an instrument of this proportion.

TONAL ADDITIONS

Several entirely new stops were added. I must emphasize that no changes in the balance of the original instrument were made to accommodate them. They are, strictly speaking, additive. That is, should a player choose to ignore the new stops, the organ can be used as it was originally specified (with the exception of the few tonal changes noted above).

The addition of a 2' flute in the Swell and a 2' principal in the Pedal on existing wind chests

was discussed previously in connection with tonal changes to the existing instrument. The other additions will be discussed in the following paragraphs.

Organ building solutions that seem ideal on paper often fail in reality. One example is clearly evident in this organ. Harrison obviously thought of the Positiv as being connected with the Choir and the Great with the Bombarde. The Choir was to provide substance and fundamental for the Positiv, and the Bombarde was to provide the first principal chorus and the reed chorus for the Great. Unfortunately, in both cases placement and acoustics defeated the plan. Additionally, it seemed difficult in practice to treat separate divisions as a unit through coupling. Therefore it was necessary to provide both the Great and the Positiv with some additional resources to make them independent.

The first addition, and the most controversial to some, was chorus reeds on the Great. Harrison had planned for Great reeds initially. A March 1945 stoplist specifies Great reeds as follows: 16' Double Trumpet, 8' Trumpet, 4' Clarion. But Harrison wrote to Schreiner on December 5, 1945, "I have from time to time looked with somewhat of a critical eye on the 16', 8' and 4' Trumpets which are included at the present time." At another point he stated, "In studying old specifications of the classic period, I have often noted a 16' Baroque reed placed on the Great organ, and have tried to imitate this in certain instances." He explained that he was very pleased with a 16' free reed Euphone at St. Mary the Virgin in New York City, and then he suggested, "Why wouldn't it be a good idea to eliminate [the Trumpets], and use the money thus saved to help pay for a 16' Euphone on the Great organ, making that a single reed on that department, and expanding our Bombarde section."

Throughout the correspondence, the Bombarde section loomed important in Harrison's mind. He was constantly pushing for it, and one wonders if he would have been most pleased to have the Great as originally specified *and* the Bombarde. On July 1, 1948, Harrison again wrote to Schreiner: "There is one thing troubles me and that is the 16' Great Euphone. The one in St. Mary's has proved itself to be unreliable. . . . Perhaps a 16' Fagotto or fairly free-toned English-type Trumpet."

Many Æolian-Skinner organs had 16' reeds on the Great, and some had reed choruses. Still, Harrison's ideal, at least at the time of the Tabernacle organ, was to depend on a massive flue chorus. It must be noted, of course, that the Bombarde division contained both a flue and a reed chorus.

Many people think that adding reeds to a G. Donald Harrison Great ruins his concept. All of us on the project felt that adding reeds, as long as they did not hamper in any way the existing Great, could not possibly harm the organ. After all, the reeds simply need not be used if one is uncomfortable with them. Since the inclusion of a substantial reed chorus on organs of nearly all traditions and nearly all periods is normal, we felt that it did the Tabernacle organ an injustice not to have this capability in service of the great organ literature.

The difficult question was what kind of reeds these should be. Our concept was to provide what many organ builders call "normal trumpet tone." We wanted to avoid all extremes, since the musical purpose was to provide timbre and volume of trumpet tone in between the Swell and Bombarde. We started by providing a 16' much like Harrison provided on other instruments. The 8' and 4' registers had progressively increasing scales. All of the

shallots are slightly tapered and slightly closed. The bells are made of tin with zinc in the stems of the basses. The boots are of thick common metal. This reed chorus has been one of the most useful additions to the instrument. It adds another dimension in character and dynamic and allows the Great, for the first time, to stand fully on its own. The new reeds have added colorful solo possibilities, and the 16' stop has been borrowed into the Pedal at both 16' and 8' to provide another dynamic terrace in the Pedal reed department. (Borrows from the Swell Contre Trompette at 16' and 8' were also added to provide still another level under expression.)

An 8' Montre was added to the Great organ. This stop has two purposes. First, it does what the Bombarde Diapason 8' was intended to do—serve as the number one principal tone of a three-level Great. Second, it is scaled in the bass to add power in the range below tenor F.

One tone character entirely missing from the Tabernacle instrument was a wide-scale 8' Cornet. We provided a five-rank Cornet on the Great and made it available as a borrow on the Antiphonal and Solo. No claim is made that the addition of such a stop will make the Tabernacle organ capable of rendering authentic performances of French classical repertoire; however, the addition of this distinct color is a remarkable enhancement and further broadens the scope of this eclectic instrument.

There is no doubt that the Positiv organ lacked foundation. Like the reedless Great, the foundationless Positiv is a concept of the mid-twentieth century that worked much better on paper than in reality. However, the concept of a weak third manual division is not solely the province of the organ reform movement. American organ building has suffered from weak Choirs as well as weak Positivs for generations. We felt that as long as future generations could hear the original G. Donald Harrison Positiv as it was conceived, it would be quite proper to add some elements to give the Positiv a proper balance within the ensemble. The organists had to depend on coupling from the Choir to provide 8' principal and reed tone. We added an 8' Principal scaled and voiced strictly in the Æolian-Skinner tradition to blend with the existing principal chorus.

The Choir Cromorne was constantly coupled but due to placement was never in balance and seldom in tune. The only Positiv reed originally was a quarter-length Rankett. We thought this stop could work very well as a sub to a dominant unison, but the unison was missing! Harrison's pre-contract stoplist called for a Cromorne on the Positiv and a Clarinet on the Choir. Later he dropped the Clarinet, moved the Cromorne to the Choir, and substituted the Rankett on the Positiv. The obvious solution was a return to the original plan for the Positiv. We provided a large-scale, French-style Cromorne. The stop is as powerful as a light trumpet. It works beautifully with the Rankett to give a reed chorus to the Positiv.

The Rankett had been softened over the years to work better as the lone reed in the division. With addition of the Cromorne, we were able to bring it back to its normal, comfortable volume le el. The Rankett also had an inveterately unstable range. The pipes had been worked on so much over the years that they were in poor condition. After some additional work, we found that the chest holes were too small. These were enlarged and the damaged pipes remade. The stop is now quite successful in its whole range. This corroborates the story that the Rankett scale was changed during the manufacturing of the organ. Evidently, a special baroque-style reed had been developed

by Oscar Pearson, and the chest was made for it. The stop did not prove successful, so a more normal quarter-length, fagott-style reed was substituted and called Rankett. The bass chest had very large racks that were adapted, and the treble range, obviously, was intended for smaller pipes.

The final additions were a pair of new reed stops on high wind pressure. Many who have played and heard the Tabernacle organ have felt that it lacked a final crowning glory of reed power. The first thought, naturally, was a Trompette *en chamade*. Another appealing thought was a smooth but glowing Willis-style Tuba that could carry a solo line over full Swell. After much effort in making a choice, we decided to include them both.

Since stops of this nature can often do more harm than good to a fine instrument, tremendous study was put into the style and placement of these prominent stops. Sample pipes were made, along with a special high-pressure test wind system and chest. Both Trompette and Tuba samples voiced at various wind pressures were tried in all possible locations in the organ and in various trajectories from horizontal to vertical. We immediately eliminated the idea of mounting *en chamade*. In the Tabernacle the best effect is achieved by using the domed shape of the ceiling to distribute the sound. We finally settled on a Tuba Mirabilis, scaled after the original Æolian-Skinner Solo Tuba but played on 15" wind pressure and located in the lower left front of the case, and a Trompette Harmonique, scaled to complement the Bombarde Trompettes and on 12" wind pressure located in the lower right front of the case in front of the Bombarde.

The Æolian-Skinner Bombarde Trompettes 8' and 4' were originally slated to be mounted horizontally (*en chamade*). The 8' and 4' along with the added 16′ were installed hooded. (The records do not indicate reasons for this change, but we may assume that they could have been financial or logistical or both.) In any event, the final result was somewhat unfortunate. This now has been corrected by the Trompette Harmonique, which, when drawn with the Bombarde reed chorus, adds a remarkable amount of fundamental and solidity.

It is a real luxury to have two marvelous Tubas, one under expression and one open. In volume level, both of the new reeds are just slightly above the Bombarde and are telling, but not in the slightest overwhelming, over the full organ ensemble and other large combinations. These stops do not violate the Harrison-Schreiner ideal of restraint in dynamic levels.

WIND SYSTEM

The wind system of this instrument is unusual among Æolian-Skinner organs. Most manual chests are fed by double-rise, weighted reservoirs rather than the normal spring-loaded, single-fold type. Harrison was obviously calling on his experience in England as we see from this quotation in a letter to Aubrey Thompson-Allen, dated February 1, 1949:

> The Salt Lake City organ is now all finished, accepted and paid for, and it is really a grand job of its kind. Probably coming from England an instrument of this type will be quite a shock to you as it is a far cry from anything one hears in England or on the Continent for that matter. When you have an opportunity to look it over there are many features that will seem like old friends, such as the double-rise reservoirs which I used for all manual departments, together with the time-honored concussion valves.

As an aside, Harrison must have felt that this instrument should stand above other Æolian-Skinners. We speculate that he took the very finest English cathedral organs as a model. Another example was his specification that

nearly all reeds should be hooded—a common practice in first-class English instruments.

The weighted, double-rise reservoirs also helped us in a very important part of our research. Establishing proper wind pressures in a restoration creates a quandary for the restorer. Many factors can change over the years, but springs add to the confusion because they can become weak and are easily mixed up from reservoir to reservoir or mounted with differing degrees of tension. Careful inspection indicated that the weights of the reservoirs had remained in place over the years, so we felt quite confident in retaining the pressures as we found them in all cases, except the Solo Tuba.

Unfortunately the "time-honored concussion valves" were not applied very liberally, resulting in the unsteady wind mentioned above. Some of the winkers in place were not properly positioned nor of a design that allowed enough flexibility to absorb shocks in the system. Additional units were added throughout the instrument, especially in the Bombarde and Solo, and resulted in an excellent improvement—probably what Harrison had hoped for.

To solve the minor deficiency in wind that caused flatting on full organ, the primary Pedal-bass wind system was separated and fed by an added 3 horsepower Spencer turbine blower. The separation also helped steady the other divisions. Evidently there was always a bit of worry on Schreiner's part about the capacity of the blower. On December 5, 1945, Harrison wrote to Schreiner, "We will, of course, check up on the horsepower of the blower before it is ordered, although I feel certain that it is still plenty large enough."

ELECTRICAL SYSTEM

The original electric-pneumatic key relays had been changed to telephone-type units. The equipment was not up to professional organ building standards and was beginning to fail. The original Æolian-Skinner switches were ready for rebuilding. We decided to replace the entire relay and switching system with solid-state equipment. The system was designed and installed by H. Ronald Poll and Associates of Salt Lake City, working closely with the in-house maintenance staff. The equipment and engineering were provided by Solid State Logic of England. Provisions for all added stops were incorporated as specified by us. Now the entire system, which is a most complicated one, including numerous couplers, chest cut-outs, and offset chest switches, is contained in a space that is about 10 percent of the original. The system is easily accessible for service and contains no moving parts.

CONSOLE

It was decided to do a complete console rebuild, renewing everything, even those components such as combination action leather that had several years of operating life left. The console had to be removed to our factory for this work, and it seemed practical to do everything in one step. Since the Tabernacle organ had to be kept in use at all times, a temporary four-manual console was built by R. A. Colby of Johnson City, Tennessee, under the direction of H. Ronald Poll and Associates of Salt Lake City, who installed it. This temporary console also facilitated the installation and switch-over to the new electrical system without missing a single daily recital or weekly choir broadcast and performed excellent service for eighteen months while the original console was refurbished. The day the Æolian-Skinner console was removed, the new console was already operating. Through the use of connectors, this same fast exchange took place when the original console was reinstalled.

The Æolian-Skinner console was sent to San Francisco in November 1985 and stripped down to bare wood. Every component was rebuilt, and the case and both benches (the original Æolian-Skinner bench and a second bench of a more open design for the purposes of television) were refinished. Over the years the case had been damaged in thousands of stage setups. Missing parts of delicate carvings and moldings, broken corners, and other parts were remade along with a new nameboard. The original two-tone finish (different woods and degrees of sheen on the case and in the jamb/nameboard area) was duplicated.

Several new features were added to the console, including an adjustment device for the music rack, built-in communications equipment for organ service and rehearsal, timers, signals and other equipment necessary to produce the weekly broadcast, and all of the controls for the solid-state equipment. Since the Tabernacle is not air conditioned, the organists used to get very hot under the television lights. We built a fan into the console with adjustable ducts. Thus this may be the only "air-conditioned" console in the world! Many of these conveniences had been added over the years as extra items attached externally to the console, somewhat marring its stately appearance. Everything was built in and hidden as much as possible in the 1988 renovation.

We also added some console controls for more flexibility. For example, duplicate general pistons were provided on the right side of the key slips, and duplicate pedal thumb pistons were added. Some toe studs and toe levers were added as space permitted. A reverser to exchange Manual I and Manual II was provided to accommodate the French system of divisional relationships.

In all of these modifications to the console, we had one guiding principle: to maintain the elegant simplicity of which Harrison and Schreiner were so proud when the organ was designed. It should be noted that the couplers are on knobs in the jambs, and that the console does not bristle with countless toe studs and controls. We added only those items that we felt were absolutely necessary and took special pains to conceal all modern controls that were not of the original Æolian-Skinner style. For example, we made Skinner-style bezels for all of the new solid-state indicators, broadcast signals, and timers and spread them discretely across the nameboard. We made a sliding drawer under the key desk to contain all of the auxiliary solid-state controls and a duplicate sliding drawer on the opposite side of the console to store pencils, papers, and other items that clutter most consoles. The memory selector and crescendo selector were located on thumb pistons on the key slips. One especially interesting task was creating a special illuminated "on-the-air" indicator using a type style for the logo that was in use by the Columbia Broadcasting System in 1948! We also replaced fluorescent lights with incandescent ones on dimmers and took special care to make every detail of the console consistent with the Æolian-Skinner tradition.

New stop-knob assemblies were exact copies of the originals with many parts, including the knob heads, furnished by the same suppliers used by Æolian-Skinner. The knob stems were hand-turned in ebony. The knobs were engraved by Hesco in the original style. Balanced pedals, toe studs, toe levers, and other controls were rebuilt or replaced using duplicates made by Harris Precision Products. The pedalboard was completely rebuilt with new natural covers and sharp caps.

We carefully studied the manual keyboard situation and decided to replace rather than rebuild. The second set of Æolian-Skinner keyboards, installed about 1960, was not of the same high quality as the original set. Rather than attempting to replace these, we thought it best to start afresh. We engaged P & S Organ Supply of Brandon, Suffolk, England, to make exact replicas of the keys and thumb pistons. We started by purchasing a two-manual set to try in the Tabernacle environment. These test keys went through the change of seasons with flying colors. We then sent all five Æolian-Skinner manuals to England so the painstaking job of measuring and tooling up could begin. The new keys were custom made to the original models. The original nameplates were retained. The finished keys look and feel like the Skinner originals but have many design improvements that make them easy to regulate and rebuild in the future. They are elegant and are of the very highest standards of workmanship. The Æolian-Skinner keyboards have been retained and fitted by the Tabernacle organ technicians as spares to be used in the future whenever the new keyboards need to be refurbished. The console was returned home in time for the 3,000th broadcast of "Music and the Spoken Word" on February 15, 1987.

COMBINATION ACTION

Replacing the remote Æolian-Skinner combination action with a solid-state unit was a difficult decision. Whereas the original Æolian-Skinner relay was gone, the combination action was still in place and functioning well, given its age. The arguments of originality and reliance on time-proven technology are strong ones for preserving this equipment. On the other hand, the reduced maintenance cost, flexibility, and multiple memory capability of solid-state combination action are appealing.

In the case of the Tabernacle organ, the decision was weighted by the use the instrument receives. It is played in recital every day of the year, sometimes twice daily. It is used for Tabernacle Choir rehearsals and a weekly worldwide live radio broadcast. There are three full-time staff organists and two associate organists plus guest organists throughout the year. Practice time is limited by other activities in the Tabernacle, including regular tours. It seemed to us that if any organ could benefit from a multiple-memory combination action, this one could. Furthermore, and of great importance to admirers of Æolian-Skinner consoles, the combination action was remote, and therefore there would be no difference in feel of the knob motion. The original pneumatically operated knobs could be retained. Therefore, it was decided to substitute a Solid State Logic 64-level combination action with the potential of expansion to 256 memory levels. Many other features possible with a solid-state combination action were also incorporated into the console. The equipment, made by Solid State Logic, was designed and installed by H. Ronald Poll and Associates.

MECHANICAL REBUILDING

We will not dwell here on the subject of normal mechanical rebuilding—primarily releathering. Since the organ was installed, the Tabernacle has maintained a staff of in-house organ technicians who regularly tune the organ and take care of all mechanical maintenance problems as they arise. Despite the immense size and complexity of this instrument, it is safe to say that every note and every action is working at all performances. Whenever a problem is found, it is usually corrected within a few hours. It is a tribute to the craftsmanship and the materials employed in the organ's original construction that it has had very few problems over the years. Most problems have occurred in the relay, combination action, and console. These have been the subjects of recent work. Nearly all of the reservoirs have been releathered during last few years. Most of the wind chests, including note pouches, key primaries, and stop actions, are operating on original leather that is projected to serve for many more years. Chests will be releathered by the Tabernacle organ shop as needed. Swell engines, tremulants, concussion bellows, and other devices are being rebuilt as needed.

REGULAR TUNING AND ADJUSTMENT

We have worked closely with the Tabernacle maintenance crew on procedures for continuing care of the instrument. Particular attention has been placed on proper routines for care of reed pipes. Robert Poll and his associate Lamont Anderson follow a meticulous tuning schedule throughout the year, minimizing shifts in pitch. This is accomplished through careful monitoring of temperature and humidity. Since the Tabernacle is not air conditioned, maintaining consistant temperature and humidity is difficult. Humidity variations are particularly hard on the Tabernacle instrument. Every effort is made by the Tabernacle staff to maintain good conditions for the organ.

The process of servicing and tuning any organ is aided greatly by having the proper facilities. All of the lighting in the organ chambers has been changed from incandescent to fluorescent to provide for cooler and more evenly distributed work light. An advanced, hands-free intercommunication system has been perfected so that there is relaxed, easy communication. Anyone who has struggled with tuning, tonal regulation, and mechanical adjustments on a large instrument can attest to the value of such items.

CONCLUSION

We trust that this complete résumé of the
1988 renovation will help future historians.
Working with this instrument was a constant
source of inspiration and gratification. We
hope the results of the cooperative efforts of so
many artisans would be appreciated by the
original creators of this great work of art,
including Alexander Schreiner and G. Donald
Harrison.

© 1988, *The American Organist*
Revised 1990

LOCATION OF ORGAN PIPES

LEFT	CENTER	RIGHT
Upper level: *Choir*	*Upper level:* *Great, Positiv (front)* *Swell (rear)*	*Upper level:* *Bombarde*
Lower level: *Choir*	*Lower level:* *Great, Pedal (front)* *Swell (rear)*	*Lower level:* *Solo*
Façade: nonspeaking	*Façade: Montre 32′* *(6 largest pipes)*	*Façade: nonspeaking*
(Tuba Mirabilis *immediately behind façade)*	*plus 4 side pipes)* *others nonspeaking*	*(Trompette Harmonique* *immediately behind façade)*

Remaining pedal pipes are located at the extreme back and sides. (Antiphonal is
located behind the grilles at the opposite end of the Tabernacle balcony.)

Appendix B: The Tabernacle Organ, 1990; An Annotated Stoplist

Æolian-Skinner *Opus 1075*
147 Voices, 206 Ranks, 11,623 Pipes

GREAT ORGAN
(unenclosed) Manual II
29 Voices, 44 Ranks, 2564 Pipes
Wind Pressures 3 1/2″, 3 7/8″, 4 9/16″, 4 7/8″

		Pipes
16′	Subprincipal	61
16′	Quintaten	61
8′	Principal	61
8′	Diapason	61
8′	Montre	61[1]
8′	Bourdon	61
8′	Spitzflöte	61
8′	Flûte Harmonique	61[1]
8′	Bell Gamba	61
5 1/3′	Grosse Quinte	61
4′	Principal	61
4′	Octave	61
4′	Koppelflöte	61
4′	Flûte Octaviante	61[1]
4′	Gemshorn	61
3 1/5′	Grosse Tierce	61
2 2/3′	Quinte	61
2′	Super Octave	61
2′	Blockflöte	61
1 3/5′	Tierce	61
1 1/7′	Septiéme	61
2 2/3′	Full Mixture—IV Ranks	244
2′	Fourniture—IV Ranks	244
1 1/3′	Kleine Mixtur—IV Ranks	244
1′	Acuta—III Ranks	183
8′	Cornet—V Ranks (f-f[3])	185[1]
16′	Double Trumpet	61[1]
8′	Trumpet	61[1]
4′	Clarion	61[1]
	Positiv on Great	

SWELL ORGAN
(enclosed) Manual III
29 Voices, 40 Ranks, 2561 Pipes
Wind Pressures 4 1/4″, 4 7/8″

		Pipes
16′	Lieblich Gedeckt	68[2]
16′	Gemshorn	68
8′	Geigen Principal	68
8′	Gedeckt	68
8′	Claribel Flute	68[2]
8′	Flauto Dolce	68
8′	Flute Celeste TC	56
8′	Viole de Gambe	68

8′	Viole Celeste	68
8′	Orchestral Strings—II Ranks	136
8′	Salicional	68
8′	Voix Celeste	68
4′	Prestant	68
4′	Fugara	68
4′	Flauto Traverso	61
2 2/3′	Nazard	61
2′	Octavin	61
2′	Hohlflöte	68[1]
2 2/3′	Cornet—III Ranks	183
2 2/3′	Plein Jeu—VI Ranks	366
1 1/3′	Plein Jeu—IV Ranks (from Plein Jeu VI)[1]	
2/3′	Cymbale—IV Ranks	244
32′	Contra Fagot	61
16′	Contre Trompette	61
8′	1ère Trompette	68[1]
8′	2ème Trompette	61
5 1/3′	Quinte Trompette	61
4′	Clairon	61
8′	Hautbois	68
8′	Voix Humaine (W.P. 5″)	68
	Tremulant	
	Swell to Swell 4′ (only affects stops with top octave extensions)	
	Swell to Swell 16′	

POSITIV ORGAN
(unenclosed) Manual I
16 Voices, 21 Ranks, 1257 Pipes
Wind Pressure 2 5/8″

		Pipes
8′	Principal	61[1]
8′	Cor de Nuit	61
8′	Quintade	61
4′	Principal	61
4′	Nachthorn	61
2 2/3′	Nazard	61
2′	Principal	61
2′	Spillflöte	61
1 3/5′	Tierce	61
1 1/3′	Larigot	61
1′	Sifflöte	61
1 1/7′	Septerz—II Ranks	98
1′	Scharf—III Ranks	183
1/2′	Zimbel—III Ranks	183
16′	Rankett	61
8′	Cromorne	61[1]
	Tremulant	

---

[1] Added as part of renovation project, 1984–88.
[2] Retained from earlier Tabernacle organs.
[3] Added in 1979.

CHOIR ORGAN
(enclosed) Manual I
18 Voices, 24 Ranks, 1536 Pipes
Wind Pressure 4 3/4"

		Pipes
16'	Gamba	68
8'	Principal	68
8'	Concert Flute	68
8'	Viola	68
8'	Viola Celeste	68
8'	Dulcet—II Ranks	136
8'	Kleine Erzähler—II Ranks	124
4'	Prestant	68
4'	Zauberflöte	68
4'	Gambette	68
2'	Piccolo Harmonique	61
2 2/3'	Carillon—III Ranks	183
2 2/3'	Sesquialtera—II Ranks (from Carillon)[1]	
1'	Fife (from Carillon)[1]	
2'	Rauschpfeife—III Ranks	183
16'	Dulzian	61
8'	Trompette	61
8'	Krummhorn	61
8'	Orchestral Oboe	61
4'	Rohr Schalmei	61
8'	Trompette Harmonique (Bombarde)[1]	
	Positiv off Choir[1]	
	Tremulant	
	Choir to Choir 4' (only affects stops with top octave extensions)	
	Choir to Choir 16'	

BOMBARDE ORGAN
(unenclosed) Manual IV
8 Voices, 18 Ranks, 1038 Pipes
Wind Pressure 6 1/8"

		Pipes
8'	Diapason	61
4'	Octave	61
2 2/3'	Grosse Cornet—IV–VI Ranks	306
2 2/3'	Grande Fourniture—VI Ranks	366
16'	Bombarde	61
8'	Trompette Harmonique (W.P. 12")	61[1]
8'	Trompette	61
4'	Clairon	61

SOLO ORGAN
(enclosed) Manual IV
11 Voices, 11 Ranks, 727 Pipes
Wind Pressure 9 5/16"

		Pipes
8'	Flauto Mirabilis	68
8'	Gamba	68
8'	Gamba Celeste	68
4'	Concert Flute	68
2 2/3'	Nazard	61[3]

		Pipes
2'	Piccolo	61[3]
1 3/5'	Tierce	61[3]
8'	French Horn	68
8'	English Horn	68
8'	Corno di Bassetto	68
8'	Tuba (W.P. 11 1/2")	68
8'	Cornet V (Great)[1]	
	Positiv on Solo[1]	
	Tremulant	
	Chimes (32 tubes, c-g[2], amplified)	
8'	Harp (49 bars, c-c[4], amplified)	
4'	Celesta (from Harp, 61 notes)	
	Solo-Bombarde to Solo-Bombarde 4' (affects all stops)	
	Solo-Bombarde to Solo-Bombarde 16'	

ANTIPHONAL ORGAN
(enclosed) Manual V
9 Voices, 11 Ranks, 720 Pipes
Wind Pressure 4 3/8"

		Pipes
8'	Diapason	68
8'	Gedeckt	68[2]
8'	Salicional	68
8'	Voix Celeste	68
4'	Principal	68
2'	Kleine Mixtur—III Ranks	183
8'	Trompette	68
8'	Vox Humana	68
8'	Tuba Mirabilis (Front Case) (W.P. 15")	61[1]
8'	Cornet V (Great)[1]	
	Tremulant	
	Antiphonal to Antiphonal 4' (affects all stops)	
	Antiphonal to Antiphonal 16'[1]	

PEDAL ORGAN
(unenclosed)
27 Voices, 37 Ranks, 1220 Pipes
Wind Pressures 3 3/8", 4 5/16", 4 1/2", 4 5/8", 6 3/16", 7"

		Pipes
32'	Montre (ext. of Great Subprincipal)	12[2]
32'	Flûte Ouverte	12[2]
32'	Contre Bourdon	12[2]
16'	Principal	32
16'	Flûte Ouverte	32
16'	Contre Basse	32
16'	Violone	32
16'	Bourdon	32
16'	Gemshorn (Swell)	
16'	Gamba (Choir)	
16'	Lieblich Gedeckt (Swell)	
10 2/3'	Grosse Quinte	32
8'	Principal	32
8'	Violoncello	32
8'	Spitzprincipal	32
8'	Flûte Ouverte	32

---

[1] Added as part of renovation project, 1984–88.
[2] Retained from earlier Tabernacle organs.
[3] Added in 1979.

8'	Flauto Dolce	32
8'	Gamba (Choir)	
8'	Lieblich Gedeckt (Swell)	
5 1/3'	Quinte	32
4'	Choral Bass	32
4'	Nachthorn	32
4'	Gamba (Choir)	
4'	Lieblich Gedeckt (Swell)	
2'	Principal	32[1]
2'	Blockflöte	32
10 2/3'	Grand Harmonics—V Ranks	160
4'	Full Mixture—IV Ranks	128
1'	Cymbale—IV Ranks	128
32'	Bombarde	32
32'	Contra Fagot (Swell)	
16'	Ophicleide	32
16'	Trombone	32
16'	Double Trumpet (Great)[1]	
16'	Contre Trompette (Swell)[1]	
16'	Dulzian (Choir)	
8'	Posaune	32
8'	Trumpet	32
8'	Double Trumpet (Great)[1]	
8'	Contre Trompette (Swell)[1]	
8'	Krummhorn (Choir)	
4'	Clairon	32
4'	Chalumeau	32
2'	Kornett	32

PERCUSSION

Chimes on Great
Chimes on Pedal
Harp on Choir
Celesta on Choir

COUPLERS

Great to Pedal
Swell to Pedal
Choir to Pedal
Positiv to Pedal
Solo-Bombarde to Pedal
Antiphonal to Pedal
Swell to Pedal 4' (affects all stops)
Solo-Bombarde to Pedal 4' (affects all stops)
Swell to Great
Choir to Great
Solo-Bombarde to Great
Antiphonal to Great
Swell to Choir
Solo-Bombarde to Choir
Antiphonal to Choir[1]
Antiphonal to Solo[1]
Great Tutti to Solo
Pedal Tutti to Swell
Swell to Great 4' (only affects stops with top octave extensions)

Choir to Great 4' (only affects stops with top octave extensions)
Solo-Bombarde to Great 16'
Solo-Bombarde to Great 4' (affects all stops)
Swell to Choir 4' (only affects stops with top octave extensions)

COMBINATIONS (64 Memory Levels[1])

General	0, 1-20

    1-5 and 11-15 duplicated by toe studs
    1-3, 5-7, and 13-15 duplicated on right side of keyboards[1]

Great	0, 1-8
Swell	0, 1-8
Choir	0, 1-8
Positiv	0, 1-6[1]
Solo-Bombarde	0, 1-8
Antiphonal	0, 1-4
Pedal	0, 1-8

    6-8 duplicated on thumb pistons under Manual I[1]

REVERSIBLES

Great to Pedal (thumb and toe)
Swell to Pedal (thumb and toe)
Positiv to Pedal (thumb)[1]
Choir to Pedal (thumb)
Solo-Bombarde to Pedal (thumb)
Antiphonal to Pedal (thumb)
Solo-Bombarde to Great (toe)
32' Bombarde (toe)
32' Flûte Ouverte (toe)[1]
32' Contra Fagot (toe)[1]
32' Contre Bourdon (toe)
Choir shades to Swell expression pedal (thumb)
Manual I/II (thumb) with indicator lights[1]
Sforzando (thumb[1] and toe) with indicator lights
    (Sforzando may be set independently for each memory level)

MECHANICALS

Swell expression
Choir expression
Solo expression
Antiphonal expression
Crescendo (4 crescendo sequences: Standard, A, B, and C. A, B, and C are adjustable from the console.[1])
Thirty segment L.E.D. Crescendo Pedal indicator[1]
Tremulants, celestes, and percussion may be programmed to cancel with crescendo pedal[1]
Crescendo and Sforzando blind check[1]
Chime volume control
Chimes forte/piano
Chime dampers on/off
Harp dampers on/off

[1] Added as part of renovation project, 1984–88.
[2] Retained from earlier Tabernacle organs.
[3] Added in 1979.

ACCESSORIES

Combination setter button
Memory lock[1]
Memory level selector (64 levels)[1]
Memory level "clear"[1]
Digital clock with mode selector, stop/start, reset, fast set, slow set, and hold controls[1]
"Stand by" and "On the Air" signals[1]
Broadcast timer[1]
Console fan on/off[1]
Technician call button
Intercom push to talk and volume controls[1]
Monitor on/off and volume controls[1]
Nauvoo Bell button (historic bell located outside the Tabernacle)

RELAY

Solid state[1]

BLOWERS

Main: 30 h.p.
Auxiliary pedal: 3 h.p.[1]
Antiphonal: 3/4 h.p.

TUNING

Equal temperament; A=440 at 74° F.

NOTES TO THE STOPLIST

The following notes detail all changes or other items of interest in connection with each speaking stop of the Mormon Tabernacle organ. If a stop is not footnoted, it is, to the best of our knowledge, exactly as it was left by Harrison in 1949 with the exception of the effects of normal aging and the resulting normal maintenance. Such normal maintenance included cleaning and tonal regulation. Every pipe in the organ was tested for proper speech, uniformity of timbre, and volume balance. Where necessary, regulation was carried out (see Appendix A). Work of this nature has not been individually footnoted. In the case of reed stops, repair work due to the effects of age and tuning was somewhat more extensive. The stops listed below were sent to the Schoenstein factory, where they were cleaned and given new tuning springs and scrolls (tongues and wedges were replaced only where originals were damaged):

Positiv	16' Rankett
Choir	8' Trompette
Swell	16' Contre Trompette
Swell	8' Trompette
Swell	4' Clairon (old 8' Harmonic Trumpet treble)

Bombarde	8' Trompette
Bombarde	4' Clairon
Pedal	2' Kornett

The solder filling that was added to the shallots of the Bombarde Trompette 8' and Clairon 4' was removed in 1988 to return these stops as closely as possible to their original timbre.

Changes in borrows, couplers, combinations, reversibles, mechanicals, and accessories, are self-explanatory.

GREAT

8' Montre. New pipes on actions prepared originally for Gt. 32' Montre (notes 1–6 and 29–61) and new Schoenstein actions (notes 7–28).

8' Flûte Harmonique. Original pipes (notes 1–12). New pipes (notes 13–61). All on new Schoenstein actions. (Original pipes 13–61 to 4' Flûte Octaviante.)

8' Bell Gamba. Originally intended to be a copy of a Roosevelt Bell Gamba. Delivered as a standard Salicional.

4' Flûte Octaviante. Original 8' Flûte Harmonique (notes 1–49). New pipes (notes 50–61). All on original 8' Flûte Harmonique actions.

2 2/3' Full Mixture.

12-15-19-22:	18 Notes
8-12-15-19:	12 Notes
1- 8-12-15:	31 Notes

2' Fourniture.

Original		Revised 1988	
15-19-22-26:	18 Notes	15-19-22-26:	18 Notes
12-15-19-22:	12 Notes	12-15-19-22:	24 Notes
8-12-15-19:	12 Notes	8-12-15-19:	12 Notes
1- 8-12-15:	12 Notes	1- 8-12-15:	7 Notes
1- 5- 8-12:	7 Notes		

Composition change only—no rescaling. Thirty-one new pipes made, following original scales. Old pipes placed in storage.

1 1/3' Kleine Mixtur.

19-22-26-29:	12 Notes
15-19-22-26:	12 Notes
12-15-19-22:	12 Notes
8-12-15-19:	12 Notes
8- 8-12-15:	13 Notes

Refinished (softened) by Æolian-Skinner in 1953. Returned to normal balance in 1988.

1' Acuta.

22-26-29:	12 Notes
19-22-26:	12 Notes
15-19-22:	12 Notes
12-15-19:	12 Notes
8-12-15:	13 Notes

---

[1] Added as part of renovation project, 1984–88.
[2] Retained from earlier Tabernacle organs.
[3] Added in 1979.

8′ Cornet V Ranks. New pipes on new Schoenstein actions.

16′ Double Trumpet. New pipes on new Schoenstein actions.

8′ Trumpet. New pipes on new Schoenstein actions (notes 1–12) and actions originally prepared for treble of 16′ Great reed (notes 13–61).

4′ Clarion. New pipes on new Schoenstein actions.

SWELL

Lieblich Gedeckt. From pioneer organ.

Claribel Flute. Former Kimball Melophone. Bass octave former Austin Clarabella.

2′ Hohlflöte. New pipes on original Voix Humaine action on Swell manual chest actions. Originally these actions were supplied by a special reservoir. They are now supplied by the main reservoir, and the original wind supply has been rerouted to the former Melos Anthropon (now Voix Humaine) wind chest.

2 2/3′ Cornet.

12-15-17:	49 Notes
8-12-15:	5 Notes
1- 8-12:	7 Notes

2 2/3′ Plein Jeu.

12-15-19-22-26-29:	12 Notes
8-12-15-19-22-26:	12 Notes
1- 8-12-15-19-22:	12 Notes
1- 8- 8-12-15-19:	12 Notes
1- 5- 8- 8-12-15:	6 Notes
1- 1- 5- 8- 8-12:	7 Notes

1 1/3′ Plein Jeu. Six-rank Plein Jeu is planted on two chests with two separate stop actions but originally was controlled by one knob. An additional knob was provided on the console to control the upper four ranks separately.

2/3′ Cymbale.

Original		Revised 1957	
26-29-33-36:	12 Notes	26-29-33-36:	12 Notes
22-26-29-33:	6 Notes	22-26-29-33:	12 Notes
19-22-26-29:	6 Notes	19-22-26-29:	6 Notes
15-19-22-26:	6 Notes	15-19-22-26:	6 Notes
12-15-19-22:	6 Notes	12-15-19-22:	6 Notes
12-15-15-19:	6 Notes	8-12-15-19:	6 Notes
8-12-15-15:	19 Notes	1- 8-12-15:	13 Notes

Some rescaling (reduction) was done, possibly in connection with the 1957 recomposition. In 1988, scales were returned to original as far as could be determined.

16′ Contre Trompette. Treble (4′ up) revoiced in the late 1970s.

8′ 1ère Trompette. New pipes on actions originally used for 8′ Harmonic Trumpet. 8′ Harmonic Trumpet treble substituted for 4′ Clarion. Bass placed in storage.

8′ 2ème Trompette. Stop originally named 8′ Trompette. No change other than nomenclature.

8′ Hautbois. Five additional reed pipes (notes G♯57 through C61) made to replace five flue pipes placed in storage. This was done to carry the reed tone to the highest possible point in the compass.

8′ Voix Humaine. In 1958, a Skinner unit chest was added to accommodate a Vox Humana from the old Kimball Assembly Hall organ. This was called Melos Anthropon. These pipes were removed in the 1988 project. The original Æolian-Skinner Voix Humaine was moved from the main chest to this chest. The wind system originally feeding the Voix Humaine on the main chest was rerouted to these actions.

4′ Clairon. Treble of former Harmonic Trumpet on Clairon actions. Bass of Harmonic Trumpet and original Clairon to storage. Harmonic Trumpet treble repaired 1988. (An attempt was made to revoice the original Clairon in the 1988 renovation, but little improvement resulted.)

POSITIV

8′ Principal. New pipes on new Schoenstein actions (notes 7–61) and on actions originally prepared for Great 32′ Montre (notes 1–6).

1 1/7′ Septerz

| Flat 21st: | 49 Notes |
| 24th: | 49 Notes |

1′ Scharf

22-26-29:	12 Notes
19-22-26:	12 Notes
15-19-22:	12 Notes
12-15-19:	12 Notes
8-12-15:	6 Notes
1- 8-12:	7 Notes

1/2′ Zimbel

29-33-36:	18 Notes
26-29-33:	6 Notes
22-26-29:	6 Notes
19-23-26:	6 Notes
15-19-22:	6 Notes
12-15-19:	6 Notes
8-12-15:	6 Notes
1- 8-12:	7 Notes

16′ Rankett. This stop evidenced serious speech problems apparently from its inception as pipes were badly damaged from efforts to correct the situation. We discovered that chest holes (notes A34–F42) were inadequate. Pipes that had been damaged were repaired, and the chest holes were enlarged. It is also interesting to note that the bass offset chest for this stop was designed for pipes of a larger scale. Whether this was an error or whether the pipes were changed before shipment or during finishing is unknown.

8′ Cromorne. New pipes on new Schoenstein actions.

CHOIR

2 2/3' Carillon.

> 12-17-22: 49 Notes
> 8-12-15: 12 Notes

2 2/3' Sesquialtera. Pipes were reracked and an extra knob provided on the console to control this section of the Carillon.

1' Fife. Pipes were reracked and an extra knob provided on the console to control this section of the Carillon.

2' Rauschpfeife

> 15-19-22: 18 Notes
> 12-15-19: 12 Notes
> 8-12-15: 31 Notes

This stop was based on a special scale developed for the 4' Principal of Ernest White's studio organ (opus 995, 1939). It resulted in a bulge of approximately nine steps at 1/4' (3") C. The pipes in this range were very unstable. In the 1988 renovation, thirteen new pipes were provided, and the scale bulge was reduced by three steps.

8' Krummhorn. Original pipes. Name changed to avoid confusion with new Cromorne added to Positiv. (Name of Pedal borrow also changed.)

BOMBARDE

2 2/3' Grosse Cornet.

> 12-15-17-19: 12 Notes
> 8-12-15-17-19: 12 Notes
> 1- 8-12-15-17-19: 25 Notes
> 1- 8-12-15: 12 Notes

Revoiced by Æolian-Skinner in 1969.

2 2/3' Grande Fourniture.

Original		Revised 1988	
12-15-19-22-26-29:	12 Notes	12-15-19-22-26-29:	12 Notes
8-12-15-19-22-26:	12 Notes	8-12-15-19-22-26:	12 Notes
1- 8-12-15-19-22:	12 Notes	1- 8-12-15-19-22:	12 Notes
1- 5- 8-12-15-19:	12 Notes	1- 8-12-15-19:	12 Notes
1- 1- 5- 8-12-15:	13 Notes	1- 8-12-15:	13 Notes

Pipes left in place but muted.

8' Trompette Harmonique. New Austin pipes on Austin actions fed by three-valve regulator.

8' Trompette. Revoiced in late 1970s. Returned to original voicing as much as possible in 1988.

4' Clairon. Revoiced in late 1970s. Returned to original voicing as much as possible in 1988.

SOLO

8' Flauto Mirabilis. To the best of our knowledge, the harmonic length pipes (wood) were cut down to normal length during the original tonal finishing process. These were left as is and carefully regulated.

2 2/3' Nazard. Casavant pipes on actions originally used for the two-rank Viole Celeste. Revoiced in 1988.

2' Piccolo. Casavant pipes (originally named Blockflöte) on Casavant action. Revoiced in 1988.

1 3/5' Tierce. Casavant pipes on Casavant action. Revoiced in 1988.

8' Tuba. Wind pressure originally specified at 15". Wind pressure noted at start of restoration was 14". After much experimentation, the pressure was reduced to 11 1/2".

Chimes. Slated for possible replacement in the future with large-scale orchestral chimes on electric action.

8' Harp. Slated for possible replacement with normal Skinner Harp.

ANTIPHONAL

8' Gedeckt. From pioneer organ.

8' Tuba Mirabilis. New Austin pipes on Austin action fed by triple-valve reservoir. Pipes are located in the main organ case.

PEDAL

32' Montre. 10 pipes from pioneer organ. Austin actions retained.

32' Flûte Ouverte. 12 pipes from pioneer organ.

32' Contre Bourdon. 12 pipes from Austin organ.

2' Principal. New pipes on chest originally provided for 2' Kornett. Kornett pipes moved to actions on chorus reed chest.

10 2/3' Grand Harmonics.

> 5-10-Flat 14-16-17: 32 Notes

4' Full Mixture. Originally 5 1/3' Full Mixture. 5 1/3' rank removed to storage. Low rank from Cymbale transferred as upper rank of Full Mixture.

Original	Revised 1988
12-15-19-22: 32 Notes	15-19-22-26: 32 Notes

1' Cymbale. Originally 1 1/3' Cymbale. Low rank moved to top rank of Full Mixture. New 1/3' pitch rank made as top rank of Cymbale

Original	Revised 1988
26-29-33-36: 32 Notes	29-33-36-40: 32 Notes

2' Kornett. Original pipes moved from flue chest to chorus reed chest on actions provided in 1948 for stop of unknown designation.

PERCUSSION

These knobs removed from their original locations within the Great, Pedal, and Choir divisions to provide room for other stops.

Appendix C: The Pipes of the "Pioneer" Organ

People often ask how many pipes still exist of the original organ built and enlarged up to 1885 by Joseph Ridges and Niels Johnson. The answer is that several sets are still in use in both the 1948 Æolian-Skinner organ in Salt Lake City and the 1915 Austin organ in Provo. While certain stops have been divided up and/or repitched and added to, and all have been revoiced to some extent, the following ranks can with reasonable certainty be ascribed to the period predating the Kimball organ of 1901:

IN THE SALT LAKE CITY TABERNACLE ORGAN

PEDAL
Montre 32', lowest 10 of former Great Open Bass (Ridges, 1867)

Flûte Ouverte 32', lowest 12 of Double Open Diapason (Johnson, 1885)

SWELL
Lieblich Gedeckt 16', former Choir Lieblich Gedackt 8' (Ridges, 1869)

[Bottom octave C♯–B also older pipes, source uncertain]

ANTIPHONAL
Gedeckt 8', probably former Swell Stopped Diapason 8' (Ridges, 1867)

[Bottom C by Kimball, due to repitching]

OTHER
In the Tabernacle organ, only two stops other than those mentioned above contain older pipes. The Swell Claribel Flute from Tenor C to the top consists of pipes from the former Kimball Solo Melophone; the bottom octave is by Austin. The bottom octave of the Pedal 32' Contre Bourdon is also by Austin.

IN THE ORGAN IN THE JOSEPH SMITH BUILDING AUDITORIUM, PROVO

GREAT
Double Open Diapason 16', from middle G upward (Johnson, 1885) [the upper portions of the 1st and 2nd Open Diapasons may also be older]

SWELL
Bourdon 16', probably former Swell Bourdon 16' (Ridges, 1867)

CHOIR (former ORCHESTRAL)
Melodia 8', probably former Choir Melodia 8' (Ridges, 1869)

Piccolo Harmonic 2', marked Solo Piccolo (Johnson, 1885)

Clarinet 8', marked Choir Clarionet (Ridges, 1869 or Johnson, 1885)

Flute Octaviente 4', possibly former Sw. Flauto Traverso (Johnson, 1885)

PEDAL
Bourdon 16', possibly former Stopped Bass 16' (Ridges, 1867)

N.B. Certain wood and zinc bass pipes (16' and 8' octaves) of newer (Austin) stops in the Provo organ may also predate 1900.

Robert Cundick (seated)
John Longhurst (standing l.)
Clay Christiansen (standing r.)

Appendix D: The Organists of the Salt Lake Tabernacle

ORGANISTS OF THE OLD TABERNACLE

Karl G. Maeser (1828-1901)

Fannie Young Thatcher (1849-1892)

Sarah Coke (1809- ?)

Orson Pratt, Jr. (1837-1903)

John M. Chamberlain (1844-1930)

ORGANISTS OF THE PRESENT
TABERNACLE

Joseph J. Daynes (1851-1920)
Organist 1867-1900

Henry E. Giles (1859-1938)
Assistant Organist 1901-1908

Katherine Romney Stewart (1875-1948)
Assistant Organist

John J. McClellan (1874-1925)
Organist 1900-1925

Edward P. Kimball (1882-1937)
Assistant 1905-1924; Organist 1924-1937

Walter J. Poulton (1884-1939)
Assistant Organist 1907-1908

Tracy Young Cannon (1879-1961)
Assistant 1909-1924; Organist 1924-1930

Moroni Gillespie (1891-1911)
Assistant Organist 1911

Alexander Schreiner (1901-1987)
Organist 1924-1977

Frank W. Asper (1892-1973)
Organist 1924-1965

Wade Naisbitt Stephens (1908-1984)
Organist 1933-1944

Roy M. Darley (1918-   )
Organist 1947-1984

Robert Cundick (1926-   )
Organist 1965-

John Longhurst (1940-   )
Organist 1977-

Clay Christiansen (1949-   )
Organist 1982-

Linda Swenson Margetts (1948-   )
Associate Organist 1984-

Bonnie Lauper Goodliffe (1943-   )
Associate Organist 1984-

INSTALLATION OF DISC
UNDER TEMPORARY COLBY CONSOLE

Appendix E: A Selected Discography of Recordings by Tabernacle Organists

ALEXANDER SCHREINER

The Great Organ at the Mormon Tabernacle (1959)
Columbia Masterworks ML 5425, XLP 48282/83, XSM 48284/85

Christmas with the Mormon Tabernacle Organ and Chimes (1964)
Columbia Masterworks ML 6037, XLP 77680/81, XSM 77682/83

Three Toccatas and Fugues (J. S. Bach)
Musical Masterworks Society MMS-32

Christmas Carols
Musical Masterworks Society MMS-38

A Christmas Recital (1953)
Concert Hall Society CHS 1198

Organ Symphony, Opus 78 (C. Saint-Saëns), with the Utah Symphony Orchestra, conducted by Maurice Abravanel (Assembly Hall organ)
Westminster Hi-Fi XWN 18722

FRANK ASPER

Mormon Tabernacle Organ Recital (1961)
Columbia Masterworks, XLP 5176/77

ROBERT CUNDICK

Robert Cundick at the Mormon Tabernacle Organ (1977)
Great American Gramophone Co., GADD-1040

JOHN LONGHURST

Mormon Tabernacle Organ (1983)
Philips, 412-217-1 (LP), 412-217-2 (CD), 412-217-4 (cassette)

ROBERT CUNDICK AND JOHN LONGHURST

A Tabernacle Organ Duo Extravaganza (1991)
Argo, 430 426-2 (CD), 430 426-4 (cassette)

Lamont Anderson
Robert Poll

Appendix F: A General Bibliography

The American Organist, Vol. 22, No. 12 (Dec. 1988). Articles on the Tabernacle organ and organists by Barbara Owen, John Longhurst, Darwin Wolford, James B. Welch, Clay Christiansen, Jonathan Ambrosino, Jack M. Bethards, and Robert Cundick.

Belnap, Parley L. "The History of the Salt Lake Tabernacle Organ" (diss., University of Colorado, 1974).

Callahan, Charles. *The American Classic Organ: Collected Letters* (Richmond, Organ Historical Society, 1990).

Cornwall, J. Spencer. *A Century of Singing* (Salt Lake City, 1958).

Hemingway, Donald W. *Utah and the Mormons* (Salt Lake City, n.d.).

Keyboard Instruments on Temple Square (Salt Lake City, 1984).

McDonald, Donald G. "The Mormon Tabernacle Organ" (thesis, Union Theological Seminary, 1952).

Ochse, Orpha. *The History of the Organ in the United States* (Bloomington, 1975).

Rushworth, Graeme. "An Organ for the Tabernacle: The Story of Joseph Harris Ridges." *The Tracker*, Vol. 24, No. 4 (1980).

Schreiner, Alexander. *Alexander Schreiner Reminisces* (Salt Lake City, 1984).

_____. "100 Years of Organs in the Mormon Tabernacle." *The Diapason* (Nov. 1967).

_____. "The Tabernacle Organ in Salt Lake City." *Organ Institute Quarterly*, Vol. 7, No. 1 (1957).

Young, Levi Edgar. *The Mormon Tabernacle with Its World-famed Organ and Choir* (Salt Lake City, 1930).

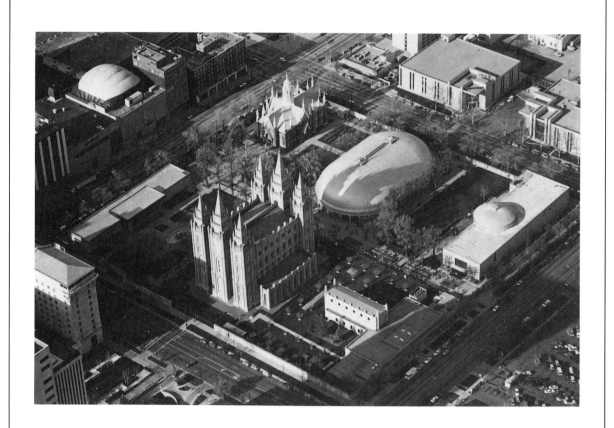

Temple Square, Salt Lake City, Utah
(Temple and domed Tabernacle in the center,
Assembly Hall above temple)

Index